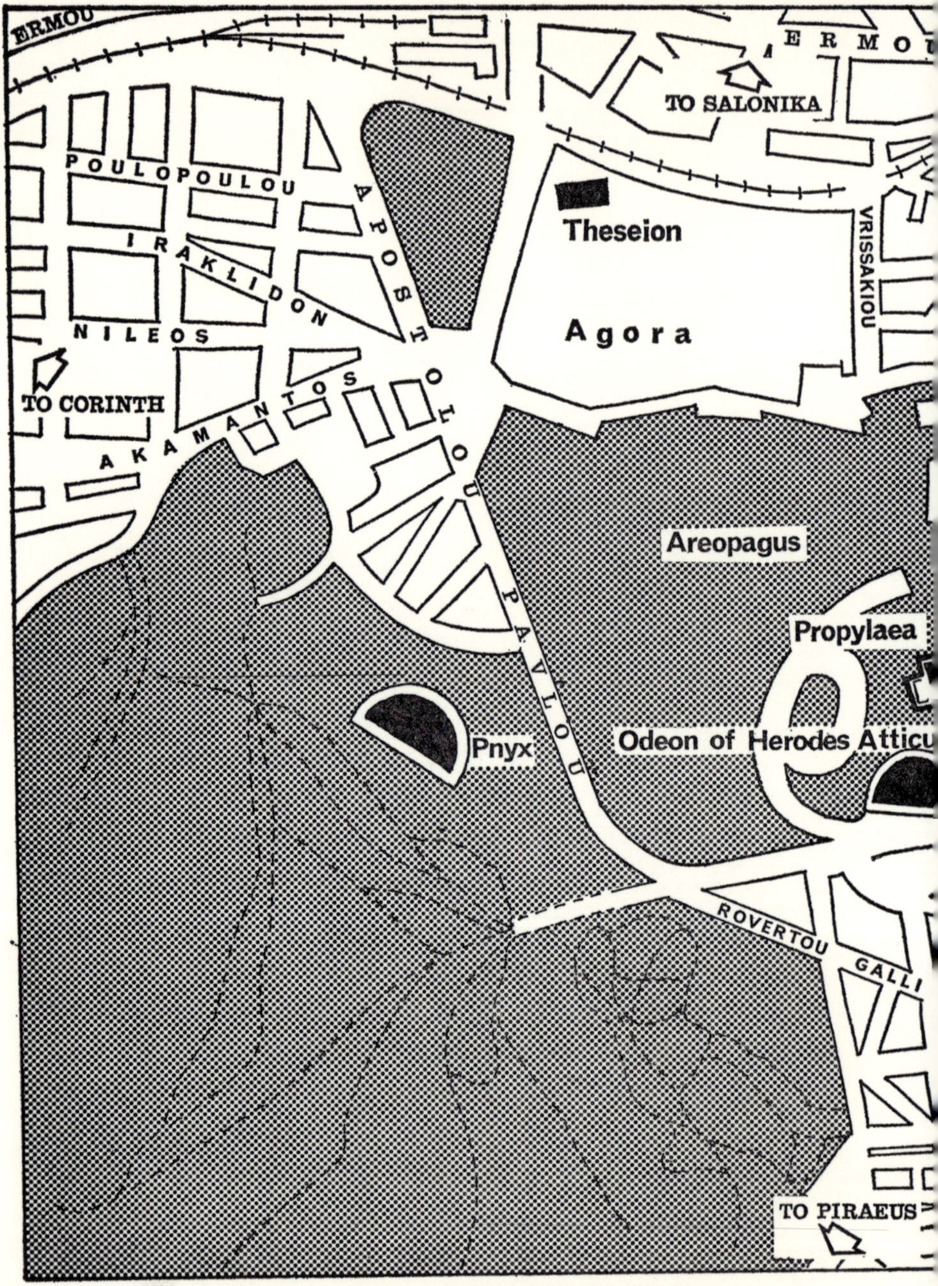

ERMOU
E R M O U
TO SALONIKA
POULOPOULOU
IRAKLIDON
NILEOS
TO CORINTH
AKAMANTOS
APOSTOLOU
PAVLOU
Theseion
Agora
VRISSAKIOU
Areopagus
Propylaea
Pnyx
Odeon of Herodes Atticu
ROVERTOU GALLI
TO PIRAEUS

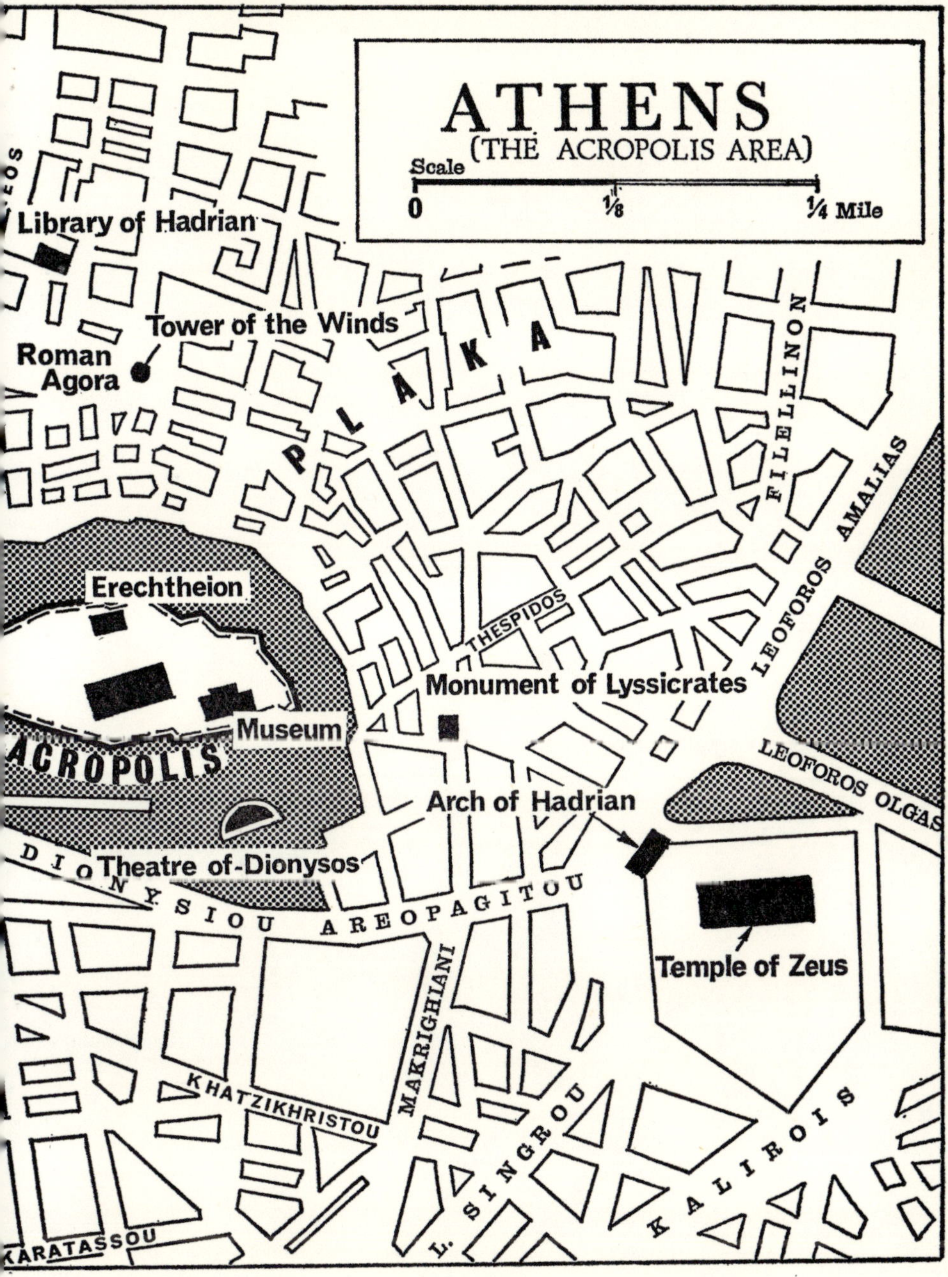
ATHENS
(THE ACROPOLIS AREA)
Scale
0
1/8
1/4 Mile
Library of Hadrian
Tower of the Winds
Roman Agora
PLAKA
FILELLINON
AMALIAS
LEOFOROS
THESPIDOS
Erechtheion
Monument of Lyssicrates
Museum
ACROPOLIS
LEOFOROS OLGAS
Arch of Hadrian
Theatre of Dionysos
DIONYSIOU AREOPAGITOU
Temple of Zeus
MAKRIGHIANI
KHATZIKHRISTOU
L. SINGROU
KALIROIS
KARATASSOU

UNKNOWN GREECE

★

Athens and the Peloponnesus

Other translations in English of the author's travel books

UNKNOWN FRANCE : FROM PARIS TO THE RIVIERA
THE FRENCH ALPS : THE RIVIERA
THE ROADS TO SPAIN
THE VALLEY OF THE LOIRE : BRITTANY

UNKNOWN SPAIN : SPAIN OF THE CONQUISTADORS (Northern Spain)
SOUTHERN SPAIN AND ANDALUSIA

UNKNOWN ITALY : THE ITALIAN LAKES AND ALPINE REGIONS
THE CITIES OF CENTRAL ITALY
SOUTHERN ITALY

UNKNOWN PORTUGAL

UNKNOWN YUGOSLAVIA

UNKNOWN SARDINIA AND UNKNOWN CORSICA

UNKNOWN SICILY

UNKNOWN TURKEY : ISTANBUL AND THE COAST OF ASIA MINOR

By Barbara Whelpton in the same series

UNKNOWN AUSTRIA:
VORARLBERG, TYROL, PROVINCE OF SALZBURG
UPPER AND LOWER AUSTRIA, VIENNA
CARINTHIA, STYRIA, BERGENLAND

UNKNOWN IRELAND

CONTENTS

UNKNOWN GREECE—VOLUME I

LIST OF ILLUSTRATIONS

21. Nemea

22. Tiryns

23. Argos—Theatre

24. Epidaurus—Theatre

25. Mistra—Metropolis

26. Mistra—Church of SS. Theodores

27. Monemvasie—St. Sophie

28. Koroni

29. Methoni—Bourzi Tower

30. Theatre of Megalopolis

31. Temple of Bassae

32. Olympia—Heraion

PREFACE

THIERRY MAULNIER remarked in his splendid book on Greece that everyone should visit the cradle of our civilization, "that Greece where we were born," at least once in his life.

In the course of an Eastern Mediterranean cruise, many people content themselves with visiting Athens, Delphi, Olympia, Mycenae, Tiryns and Epidaurus and, as far as the islands are concerned, Delos, Mykonos, Santorini in that order of importance.

Admittedly this does provide a most evocative picture of Ancient Greece and a chance to sample the charms of Modern Greece, but it is a confined condensed view of a mosaic of civilizations superimposed upon a marvellously varied terrain.

Archaic Greece is not only revealed to us at Mycenae and Tiryns; the Crete of Minos is an indispensable link in the understanding of the evolution of the human race. Even the most celebrated ancient cities have left us too often almost unrecognizable vestiges which can only awake the curiosity of archaeologists; even so it is essential to have seen Corinth, Argos, Sparta, Thebes, Dordona, Pella, and the Temple of Bassae to acquire a sufficient understanding of the civilization of classical Greece.

After Roman Greece had superseded Ancient Greece and reconstructed and redesigned its monuments, Byzantine Greece contributed some quite remarkable monuments, not only at Daphni and at Kaisariani, at the very gates of Athens, and the little churches in Athens itself, but also the monastery of Hosios Loukas near Delphi, the monasteries of the Meteora and of Mount Athos, the churches of Salonica, Mistra, Arta, Kastoria and Verroia.

All these Byzantine churches are decorated either with frescoes or with mosaics, and we must not forget the most impressive of all Byzantine churches, the monastery of Nea Moni, on the island of Chios.

We should also take into account the churches of Skripou in Boeotia, Merbaka in Argolis, Geraki, Monemvasia, Chrysapha in Laconia, Gavrolimni and Amphissa. We shall discover a great many others elsewhere.

Frankish castles and fortifications can be seen in most regions. They spread along the coast but the most remarkable are to be found at Rhodes, the island of the Knights of St. John.

The Venetian occupation has left us the surrounding walls of Chalcis, Nauplia, Acrocorinth, Monemovasia, Navarino, Methoni, Kasteri and of Karystos. Venetian walls can also be seen in Candia, in Crete, as well as the arsenals of Gouvia in Corfu and the ruins of the Venetian town of St. George in Cephalonia.

The Turks have only left us a few mosques in Athens, Nauplia, Chalcis, Canea, and Candia and some charming fountains. They also strengthened and redesigned some ancient Frankish and Venetian fortifications.

So many books have been written on the History and the Art and Architecture of Greece that I shall content myself by briefly summarizing the major periods of Art in Ancient Greece.

Art made its appearance in Greece during the course of the second millennium before Christ and from this first period we can date the Neolithic town of Dymini in Thessaly with its series of surrounding walls, the Palace of Lerne in Argolis, called the "house of tiles". This is termed the ancient Helladic.

With the arrival of the Greeks and the middle Helladic period we can see the beginnings of fortified palaces like that of Dorion-Malthi in Messena and the pottery called Minoan made with a fine micaceous clay in contrast to the glaze productions of the preceding epoch. This usually takes the form of grey or sometimes yellow vases.

The Achaian kings erected powerful fortresses in which they guarded their treasures on the crests of hills. The one at Mycenae is composed of a triangular acropolis surrounded by cyclopean walls. Within, stands the palace with its throne room, a sanctuary, a megaron preceded by two vesticles, one on the outside and one on the inside with, in the middle, a hearth surrounded by four columns and surmounted by a lantern. We find the same arrangement at Tiryns and at Pylos.

The tombs are of three successive types: vertical tombs, tombs with cells cut into the rock and tombs with cupolas (*tholos*) or an entrance with a corbelled vault of which the most typical example is the Treasury of Atreus.

Cretan influence is manifest in the decoration of these palaces. The walls, covered with frescoes, continue the Minoan tradition with a more simple design and without regard to natural colouring. Certain subjects, like the procession in the Palace of Tiryns with its two lines of women in ceremonial costume, which come towards each other on the walls of the *megaron*, are of Cretan inspiration, but, others also treated according to the Cretan style, represent, as at Mycenae, horses and warriors.

If the round boss is rare among the Mycenaeans, their reliefs in stone are expressive, like the lintel which decorates the gate of the acropolis at Mycenae with its heraldic lionesses.

Ceramics in a great variety of types, originally inspired by Crete, became stylized and the designs were reduced to rosettes and horizontal bands, whereas goldsmiths' work, torques and inlay, have left us astonishing masterpieces as is witnessed by the famous treasure found at Mycenae to which we may add cups and goblets discovered at Pylos, at Medea and at Vaphio.

Ceremonial weapons found in the tombs are just as magnificent with their hilts decorated with hunting scenes.

After the Dorian invasion, there appears at the beginning of the 10th century a proto-geometric art which keeps something of the Mycenaean tradition and oriental influences mixed with what may be considered as the contribution of the invaders. Covered with a dull glaze, vases are decorated with simple geometric patterns: circles, semicircles and triangles like those to be seen on the examples from the Cemetery of Ceramics.

The so-called Geometric Style appeared towards 900 B.C. To the geometric patterns already in use, were added the meander, the swastika and then men and animals. Very much conventionalized, the figures were depicted naked with a circle for the head, a triangle for the body and straight bands for legs. Funeral scenes, processions of chariots, choirs and dancers are represented in a diagrammatic and narrative fashion.

The first temples, which appear between 850 and 750 B.C., are rectangular buildings with a pointed roof and a porch on the façade.

Sculpture reappeared in Crete with the ritual tympanum in bronze, discovered in the cave of Ida and dating from the 9th to the 7th centuries, whilst from the 8th century the little bronzes, usually of warriors and animals, had much in common with the Geometric style of ceramics. The 7th century witnessed the beginning of working in ivory.

It was not until the Archaic period (750–500 B.C.) that art was to make any great progress in Greece and first of all in the field of architecture where the best materials were to be employed, limestone and, above all, marble, with columns skilfully cut and fitted together without the use of cement: clamps and joggles being sufficient to join the blocks.

The temple, which the god was supposed to inhabit with his statue, had only a *naos* to begin with, where the statue stood. Soon a *pronaos* was added (or a vestibule) and the *opisthodome* which was an addition at the back.

Where secret rites were involved there is a fourth room, the *adyton* or *abaton*, the inaccessible chamber at the back of the *naos* as in the temple of Apollo in Delphi.

Temples without colonnades are rare for, in the simplest types, the porch of the *pronaos* is supported by two columns between the *antae*. Later the façades were decorated with columns; these were termed *pro-style* or *amphi-prostyles*. Then the colonnade surrounded the temple on four sides, termed peripteral. It depends on the number of columns of the façade whether the temple is tetrastyle, hexastyle or octostyle.

There are a great many variations of each style but, from the period of High Archaic times, styles have been divided into Doric or Ionic orders. The first of these originated in the Peloponnesus and spread throughout the countries which came under its influence, such as Sicily and Magna Graecia. It is characterized by a more or less massive column without a base with capitals formed of a circular *echinus* and a square *abacus*. The architrave is smooth and the frieze is made up of alternating *triglyphs*, blocks carved with two channels in the centre, flanked by half channels and by *metopes*, blocks which are usually decorated with sculpture. The *soffit* of the cornice has *mutules* decorated with projecting *guttae*. This is the transformation of primitive wooden temples into stone.

The Ionic Order, which made its appearance in Greek Asia and in the islands, has a more slender column resting on a base and its capital is decorated with volutes. The architrave is composed of a triple fascia, and the frieze, when it exists, is a continuous band decorated with narrative scenes. The *soffit* of the cornice is often ornamented with serrations.

These two orders which originally symbolized the aesthetic tastes of the Dorians and the Ionians developed from simple decorative motifs used in the same building: Doric on the outside and Ionic on the inside, or Ionic superimposed upon Doric.

The Corinthian Order is a variation of the Ionic style. It

is characterized by its capital decorated with acanthus leaves and it made its appearance at the end of the 5th century B.C. Appreciation of its rich decorative qualities kept it in use throughout the 4th century and in the Hellenic period.

A sacrificial altar stands in front of the temple; this is either rectangular (*bomos*) or round (*bothros*). It is a ditch or hollow where the blood of the victim is offered to the divinities.

Important sanctuaries had, as well as treasuries, little buildings consisting of one chamber with a porch where rich offerings, usually from cities, were safeguarded.

Beyond the area devoted to religious rites, the establishments dedicated to games were just as carefully laid out. First there were the theatres which played an important role in the cult of Dionysos, and which were built in stone from the 4th century, and the gymnasium. Everyone knows what an important part physical exercise played in Ancient Greece. The stadium and the hippodrome are long tracks surrounded by tiers of seats; the gymnasium with the *pelestra* served as a training centre for athletes.

These edifices were also meeting places, like the *agora*, the public square in the centre of the city surrounded with porticoes with shops.

The most celebrated Doric temples of the archaic period are: the Heraion of Olympia, which dates from the 7th century B.C. in its final form; that of Apollo at Delphi, reconstructed at the end of the 14th century. The most famous Ionic temples are the Heraion of Samos dating from about 575, a dipteral edifice where the forest of columns recalls the hypostyle halls of the orient. Among the treasuries, the Doric treasury of Sicyone and the Ionic treasury of Cnidus (545) and of Siphnos (525) where the façade columns are replaced by caryatids.

Architecture reached its greatest heights in the 5th century. In 468 was begun the majestic Doric temple of Zeus at Olympia. Athens has the Parthenon, a Doric temple enlivened with an Ionic frieze, the temple of Athena Nike and the Erechtheum; at Eleusis is the Telesterion.

Innovations appeared from the end of the 5th century with the temple of Apollo at Phigalia designed by Ictinos, the architect of the Parthenon, at Delphi where the Temple of Apollo is reconstructed and where they erected the Treasury of Cyrenus, a synthesis of the geometric problems solved by Theosoros, the great mathematician of Cyrenus; at Epidaurus where the Argian Polyclitus the Younger built the finest of the Greek theatres; at Tegea in the temple of Alea Athena and at Gortys where the temple of Aesclepios was built by Scopas. Here the Corinthian Order outshone the others in nobility.

In the Hellenistic era it was the cities of Asia Minor, Pergamum, Ephesus, Aphrodisias which developed and further embellished it; and in the Roman era, Hadrian and Herodes Atticus constructed new buildings, but by this time decadence had already set in.

Greek sculpture, which produced so many masterpieces of art, followed a similar pattern of evolution. In the Archaic period it was simply a question of wooden carvings which have disappeared. Stone came into use at the end of the 7th century with the *kore* and the *kouros*.

The *kouros* is a young man represented standing, arms at the side, the left leg slightly forward in a pose reminiscent of Egyptian sculpture. A *kore* is a young girl draped in a tunic and a cloak, holding an offering in the right hand whilst the left holds the drapery across her thigh. They represent young initiates. There are also one or two statues of divinities such as the head of Hera at Olympia.

Doric art is more austere, more massive than Ionic art, like the twins of Delphi, Kleobis and Biton, the work of an Argian sculptor, whereas Ionian art, which developed in the islands, pleasanter, more delicate and rhythmic, is exemplified by the maidens of Delos with their finely pleated chitons in contrast to the large pleats of the *himation* of wool. In Athens the two tendencies of graveness and gentleness are reconciled as in the *Grumbling Woman* and the *Fair Ephebus*.

Sculptured reliefs, usually painted, decorated the pediments, the friezes and *metopes*, where separate scenes were depicted like the *Labours of Hercules*, whilst the frieze could be used to illustrate a continuous narrative as in the treasury of Siphnos where there are four episodes: *The Judgement of Paris*, *The Abduction of Hippodamia*, *The Fight before Troy*, and *The Wars of the Giants*.

From the end of the 6th century, sculpture evolved towards a more natural representation of the human body and faces become more expressive, but it was after the wars of the Medes and Persians that classical sculpture appeared exemplified by the *Poseidon* of Cape Artemision and the *Auriga* of Delphi.

Architectural sculpture is exemplified in the decoration of the Temple of Zeus at Olympia where the *metopes* depict the exploits of Hercules and where the façades show two scenes of impressive nobility; the preparation for the race between Pelops and Aenonaes and the battle of the Centaurs and the Lapiths.

Classicism attained its highest level with the next generation; Myron, Polyclitus and Phidias, to whom we owe the statue of *Athena Parthenos* and the decoration of the Parthenon with the four Doric friezes dedicated to *The Wars of the Giants*, *The Taking of Troy*, *The Wars of the Amazons*, *The Wars of the Centaurs* which symbolized the triumph of reason over chaos, whilst *The Birth of Athena* and *The Dispute of Attica* between Athena and Poseidon occupy the two pediments. On the Ionic frieze, we see the procession of the Panathenians with the crowd coming to render homage to the gods.

At Eleusis, Phidias shows us Demeter and Core giving back to the young Triptolemus the ear of corn which is the embodiment of human nourishment and also holds the promise of life in the afterworld.

Among Phidias' circle new tendencies were being evolved by Alcemenes, Kresilas, Callimacus, the creator of the Corinthian capital, Paionios of Mendes.

The 4th century, more mystical and less serene, is represented by Praxiteles whose languid bodies of effeminate adolescents and naked women are rendered with incomparable grace.

Scopas of Paros expresses with violent movement the pathos of the Dionysiac trances, whereas Lysippus of Sicyone, above all else a bronze worker, elongates the lines of the figure and shows his knowledge of the human body in *The Apoxymenes*.

In the Hellenic period we see new schools prospering at Alexandria, Pergamum, Aphrodisias, as well as at Delos and at Rhodes with Chaves of Lindos, creator of the famous Colossus and a disciple of Lysippus.

It is during this period that several masterpieces such as the *Venus de Milo* and the *Victory of Samothrace*, were produced which count amongst the foremost works of Greek art.

If Greek painting has entirely disappeared leaving us only names such as Polygnotus of Thasos, Zeuxis and Apelles, we have at least ceramics of which we possess innumerable examples in vases of all shapes.

At the beginning of the Archaic period, the influence of the orient was manifested in the vases called *orientalisants* which date from the 7th century. To geometric motifs were added flowers, stars, lions, birds, sphinx and griffons, more especially at Rhodes, Corfu and Athens where depicting of the human figure continued.

In the 6th century, black figures began to be used and the representation of the human figure took the place of animals and plant forms. Among the most notable artists was Exekias who painted mythological scenes in minute detail. We must also mention the contribution of Corinth and Sparta.

Then, towards 520, came the vogue for red designs on a glazed background. Up to 460, the style is severe and Epictetos specialized in scenes of genre, notably *bacchanalia*, whereas Euphronios returned to mythology for inspiration and Prygos gives his figures a dramatic character reminiscent of Aeschylus.

In about 460, the style became more free and sought expression on several superimposed planes with a serenity which recalls Phidias. Towards 420 this flowery style is used by Meidias with graceful, but mannered, figures.

In the 4th century, the Athenian output of ceramics was exported as far as the Crimea and was popular for its scenes of gymnasia, but expressed by its precocious production a veritable decadence. It was at this time that the Greek ceramics were first produced in southern Italy.

During the Hellenic period, ceramics were no longer decorated with human figures, but with plant forms.

* * *

In this first volume we are obliged to limit ourselves to the number of monuments and sites it is possible to see. Six itineraries are devoted to the mainland of Greece, excluding Macedonia and Salonica and Epirus which will be dealt with in Volume II; two of these concern Athens, the first dealing with the main monuments of antiquity, and the second more particularly stressing the Byzantine churches.

The third itinerary deals with the places of interest around Athens, from the monastery of Kaisariani to the ruins of the temple of Cape Sounion and the sanctuaries of Brauron and of Amphiaraos.

The fourth takes us to Delphi.

The fifth and sixth make a complete tour of the Peloponnesus and we see *en route* Daphni, Eleusis, Corinth, Mycenae, Argos, Tiryns, Nauplia and Epidaurus, Lerne, Tripolis, Sparta in our fifth itinerary; Mistra, Pylos, Bassae, Olympia and Patras in the sixth.

Travelling in Greece is no longer an adventure. The roads have become for the most part excellent. The number of comfortable hotels available has increased and the welcome of the Greek people is just as cordial and warm as ever.

There are plenty of small restaurants to delight the heart of those who appreciate local colour and Greco-Turkish cooking in the oil of the country. Fish, lamb, sucking-pig and grilled or stuffed chicken are excellent and, particularly in Athens, it is the tavernas in the Plaka which are most popular, spread out over the slopes of the Acropolis. These offer all kinds of savoury dishes including *kebab*, little pieces of meat grilled Turkish fashion on skewers on a spit.

As for the red and white Greek wines, they are pleasant enough and, if the resin upsets people who are not used to it and perhaps will never become so, there are the vintages of Tegea, Achaia, Attica, Cephalonia, Santorini, Naoussa and, as desert wines, those of Samos and Mavrodaphni.

Everyone should try, particularly as an aperitif, the ouzo and the mastic, the best of which is from Chios. It is flavoured with mastic gum.

Coffee is served Turkish style.

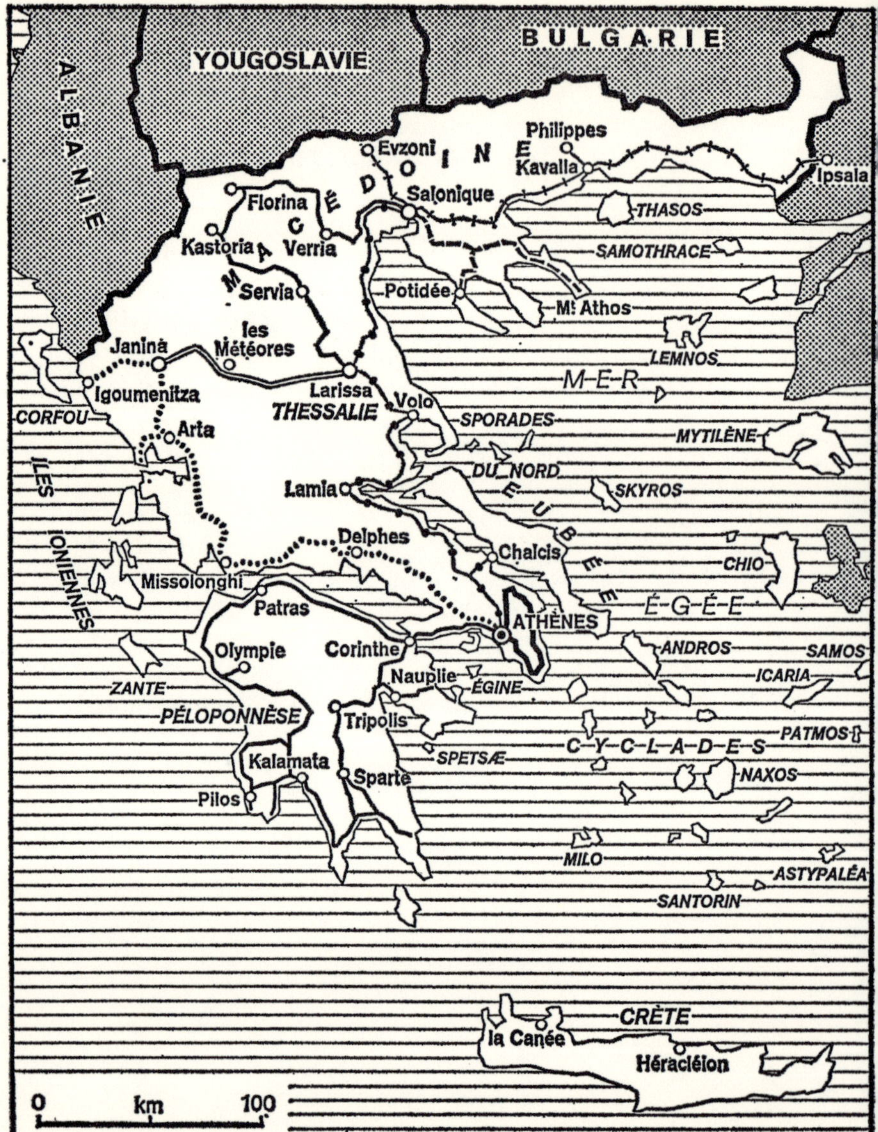

BULGARIE
YOUGOSLAVIE
ALBANIE
MACÉDOINE
Philippes
Evzoni
Kavalla
Ipsala
Salonique
Florina
Kastoria
Verria
THASOS
SAMOTHRACE
Servia
Potidée
Mt Athos
les Météores
Janina
LEMNOS
Larissa
MER
Igoumenitza
THESSALIE
Volo
CORFOU
SPORADES
Arta
MYTILÈNE
DU NORD
ILES IONIENNES
Lamia
SKYROS
EUBÉE
Delphes
Chalcis
CHIO
Missolonghi
ÉGÉE
Patras
ATHÈNES
Olympie
Corinthe
ANDROS
SAMOS
Nauplie
ZANTE
ÉGINE
ICARIA
PÉLOPONNÈSE
Tripolis
PATMOS
CYCLADES
SPETSÆ
Kalamata
Sparte
NAXOS
Pilos
MILO
ASTYPALÉA
SANTORIN
CRÈTE
la Canée
Héracléion
0 km 100

LIST OF ITINERARIES

I

ATHENS I

THE OLYMPIEION — HADRIAN'S ARCH — THEATRE OF DIONYSUS — ASCLEPIEION — ODEON OF HERODES ATTICUS — ACROPOLIS — PROPYLAEA — TEMPLE OF ATHENA NIKE — PARTHENON — ERECHTHEUM — AREOPAGUS — MOUSEION — PNYX — THESEUM — AGORA — CHURCH OF THE HOLY APOSTLES — CERAMIC CEMETERY — DIPYLON

This first itinerary in Athens includes the majority of the well-known buildings of the ancient city: those of the Acropolis, as well as those which rise round the Agora and on the neighbouring hills.

II

ATHENS II

PLAKA — MONUMENT TO LYSICRATES — TOWER OF THE WINDS — ROMAN AGORA — HADRIAN'S LIBRARY — CHURCH OF SS THEODORES — LITTLE METROPOLIS

This second itinerary is devoted to the old quarters of Athens where the small Byzantine churches neighbour ancient ruins. It is essentially complementary to the first and it will remain up to the tourist to visit the museums which will give him a complete sight of the art of ancient Greece, of both

Archaic and Classical epochs, as well as the Roman and Byzantine eras.

III

THE ENVIRONS OF ATHENS

KAISARIANI — MOUNT HYMETTUS — CAPE SOUNION — LAURION — THORIKOS — MARKOPOULO — BRAURON — MARATHON — AMPHIAREION

This itinerary includes the most interesting buildings in the environs of Athens: the monastery of Kaisariani, the Temple of Poseidon at Cape Sounion and the sanctuaries of Brauron and Amphiareion, without forgetting the sites of Rhamnonte and Marathon and the small Byzantine churches at Markopoulo and Koropi.

IV

ATHENS TO DELPHI

THE ACADEMY OF PLATO — DAPHNI — ELEUSIS — THEBES — LIVADIA — SKRIPOU — ORCHOMENUS — CHERONEA — HOSIOS LOUKAS — ARACHOVA — DELPHI

This itinerary allows us to see the ensembles *most likely to evoke our enthusiasm. First, the monastery at Daphni with its celebrated mosaics of the XI and XII centuries; and, in the realm of Byzantine churches, those of Skripou and Hosios with their admirable mosaics of the end of the X century.*

If Thebes scarcely offers us any memorable remains, at least one place merits a careful visit—Delphi, above all, for its situation and its monuments and the sculptures in its museums.

V

THE PELOPONNESUS I—MEGARA TO SPARTA

MEGARA — CORINTH — NEMEA — MYCENAE — ARGOS — MIDEA — TIRYNS — NAUPLIA — EPIDAURUS — LERNA — TRIPOLIS — TEGEA — SPARTA

This itinerary joins together the most celebrated places of the Peloponnesus which one can reach by means of excellent asphalted roads. Mycenae and Tiryns with their Cyclopean walls and their tombs; and also the palaces of Lerna. In fact, all the most celebrated cities of ancient Greece; Corinth and its Temple of Apollo; Epidaurus with its theatre; Sparta which has only its memories to offer us.

VI

THE PELOPONNESUS II—MISTRA TO SICYON BY WAY OF OLYMPIA

MISTRA — MONEMVASIA — GYTHION — AREOPOLIS — KALAMATA — KORONI — PYLOS — METHONI— MESSENA — MEGALOPOLIS — KARYTAINA — BASSAE — OLYMPIA — GASTOUNI — ANDRAVIDA — CHLEMOUTSI — KYLLINI — PATRAS — MEGASPILAION — SICYON

The southern and western part of the Peloponnese introduce us to interesting Byzantine remains as well as bringing us memories of the Turks and the Venetians. Byzantine churches are in evidence at Mistra, at Merbuka and at Gastouni. We must not forget the ancient Frank or Venetian fortresses on

Monemvasia, this peninsula where one feels oneself so distant from the real world. Also at Koroni, at Methoni and Chlemoutsi which give us another aspect of Grecian history, until now little known.

We include extensive remains of Olympia in our itinerary and also the Temple of Bassae, almost intact in its proud isolation.

ITINERARY I

ATHENS I

The Olympieion — Hadrian's Arch — Theatre of Dionysus — Asclepieion — Odeon of Herodes Atticus — Acropolis — Propylaea — Temple of Athena Nike — Parthenon — Erechtheum — Areopagus — Mouseion — Pnyx — Theseum — Agora — Church of the Holy Apostles — Ceramic Cemetery — Dipylon.

THIS first itinerary deals with the most important monuments of Ancient Athens. We begin with THE OLYMPIEION to the south-east of the Acropolis, the sanctuary of Olympian Zeus of which 15 columns remain to show its gigantic proportions.

It rises up on a site of another temple dedicated to the same god towards 515 B.C. Between the surrounding wall of the temple and the Leoforos Olgas, drums of the colossal columns of the unfinished archaic temple have been found. The construction of the temple which succeeded it was taken in hand by the Seleucid King of Syria, Antiochus IV Epiphanes, between 175 and 164 B.C. and completed by the Emperor Hadrian who consecrated it in A.D. 131.

The Roman architect Cossutius, to whom Antiochus had entrusted the work, enlarged the plan, modified the orientation, adopted the Corinthian Order and chose Pentelic marble for his material.

We can make out the ruins of houses of the 4th century B.C.

and the remains of Roman baths of the 2nd century B.C., before reaching the Propylaeum, the monumental entrance to the Olympieion which has been partly reconstructed.

The Olympieion was a dipteral temple with 2 rows of 20 columns on the sides, with 3 rows of 8 columns on the façades which make a total of 104 columns of which only 16 subsist, one of which is on the ground.

Near the Propylaeum the ruins of a basilica have been laid bare; it has 3 naves constructed with the materials from the Olympieion.

We now reach the ARCH OF HADRIAN, built in the 2nd century B.C. on the site of a former gateway in the 6th-century wall. Constructed of Pentelic marble, it is composed of a Corinthian portico under a great semicircular arch.

Next we proceed to the SACRED ENCLOSURE OF DIONYSUS ELEUTHEREUS, with the surrounding wall preserved in some places. It comprises an altar, 2 temples and the theatre of Dionysus.

The second temple of Dionysus Eleuthereus was built towards 420 and only its foundations remain. It was composed of a projecting *pronaos* and a *cella* which sheltered the chryselephantine statue of the bearded and seated god, the work of the sculptor Alcemenes.

On the right, a beautiful round Dionysian altar of marble dates from the 2nd century B.C., and is decorated with masks, satyrs, garlands and rosettes. Further on, the blue limestone foundations of the first temple built in the 4th century under Pisistrates still subsist. Smaller than the new temple, it used to contain the *xoanon* of the God which was brought from Eleutheros and carried in procession during the rites.

Nearby, the buildings of the 4th-century THEATRE OF DIONYSUS comprise an open portico to the south which masks the back wall of the wing and the wall which supports the orchestra platform.

The stage was made up of a rectangular room almost 50

metres long by 8 deep, with, on the sides, 2 projecting rooms with façades decorated with 6 Doric columns. The *proscenium* of 2 to 3 metres in height was ornamented with a colonnade in the Hellenic era.

The sculptures of the *proscenium* date from the 1st century of our era. Their subjects deal with the legend of Dionysus. We see first the Birth of Dionysus with Hermes standing holding the newborn before the seated Zeus, whilst two Corybantes carry out a war dance. Then there is a scene of sacrifice in honour of Dionysus with Icarus and a peasant initiated by Dionysus in the cultivation of the vine and the making of wine; he approaches the altar leading a goat. To the right, Dionysus, followed by a young Satyr, offers the vine to a kneeling Silenus. Next we see, in *The Homage of the Gods and of the Attic city to Dionysus*, the god seated on a throne with, above him, the Parthenon and moving in procession towards him Hestia, Theseus, Eirene (Peace) with a cornucopia, etc.

Between the stage and the tiers of seats are the principal entrances flanked by statues and votive monuments. In early times, when there was not yet a stage, choirs performed in the orchestra, for the present paving dates from the reign of Nero or of Hadrian. A great lozenge marks the site of the altar of Dionysus.

The parapet which surrounds the orchestra dates from the Roman era. It protected the spectators when gladiators were fighting in the theatre. The *cavea*, almost semicircular in shape, had 78 tiers divided into 3 zones by 2 concentric terraces; each of these was hollowed out into a groove for the feet of the spectators of the row above and for the draining away of rainwater. In the 4th century, the first row was reserved for 50 prytanes, for the archons and for the priests. Most of the 67 seats of honour with backs in this row date from the Roman era and may perhaps be copies of 4th-century seats. The main place of honour in the centre was reserved for the priests of Dionysus Eleuthereus, and his marble throne has a graceful decoration of archaic bas-reliefs. Hadrian's imperial loggia was on the central axis. Imperial statues, parts of whose bases still subsist, stood in the middle of each *cuneus*. Other statues of tragic or comic poets and of musicians were disposed here and there.

To the west, the ODEON OF PERICLES has been cleared of rubbish. It was built in 443 and reconstructed in 65 B.C. thanks to the generosity of Ariobarzanes II, King of Cappadocia, and was considered to be the most beautiful concert hall of the Greek world.

From the upper terrace of the theatre we can have direct access to the ASCLEPIEION by following a path which leads to the grotto of the Panaghia Spiliotissa which still has the remains of Byzantine paintings and near which we can see two Roman Corinthian columns which supported the choragic tripods.

The cult of Asclepios, the Aesculapius of the Romans, the original god of medicine of Epidaurus, was introduced into Attica after the Peace of Nicaea during the great mysteries of 420 B.C. A first sanctuary constructed by a rich Athenian property owner was completed towards the middle of the 4th century B.C. by a second sanctuary. Each had a temple with an altar, a portico which served as a dormitory where the patients lay to wait the nocturnal appearance of the god, and a sacred spring where the sick purified themselves by ablutions before proceeding for incubation under the portico. The 5th-century sanctuary was to the west and the other to the east of the terrace.

The best preserved building is the long portico of the new Asclepieion which extended to the north of the ruins of the altar and the temple. It is to be found between a grotto with a little spring and a small raised terrace where there is a hollowed-out altar covered by an *aedicule* whose roof is supported by 4 columns.

1. ATHENS : THE OLYMPIEION.

2. ATHENS : THE PARTHENON.

The portico is composed of a colonnade of 17 Doric columns and of 2 interior galleries. It has an upper storey which is reached by a stairway to the east. The stylobate is well preserved. This *stoa* which dated from the middle of the 4th century was refashioned in the Roman era. According to legend it was here that the son of Poseidon, Halirrhothios, seduced Alkippa, daughter of Ares who killed him near the spring. The grotto was converted into a chapel by the Byzantines.

The old Asclepieion is in a far more ruined state, but there is also a portico, a temple, the remains of an altar and a spring formed from a cistern which is polygonal in shape.

By retracing our steps as far as the theatre, we shall find, to the west, the ruins of the choragic monument of Nicias built towards 320 B.C.

The portico of Eumenes was built by Eumenes II, King of Pergamum, to serve as a promenade for the theatre audience. It was then joined to the ODEON OF HERODES ATTICUS, built in A.D. 161 to serve as an all-season theatre and concert hall.

The façade is made up of a central body of two storcys and of two wings with three storeys decorated with semicircular arches and with alcoves in one of which there is still a statue of the Roman magistrate.

The stage was covered with a wooden floor and the *proscenium*, surmounted by a balustrade, was faced with marble. Three stairways, cut into the balustrade, allowed the orchestra to reach the stage. The back and the sides of the stage, pierced with doors, are decorated with a colonnade framing alcoves filled with statues which support a kind of balcony whose attachments are still visible.

The orchestra is paved with slabs of white marble and cipolin from Karystos and encircled by a gutter. The *cavea* is surrounded by a circular, buttressed wall. The 32 rows of seats could hold 5,000 spectators.

We now climb up to the ACROPOLIS which looks like a natural fortress. It is also the base on which the most pure and perfect monuments left to us by the ancient Greek civilization are built. It had indeed been a fortress from the Mycenaean era, when towards the 15th century B.C. it was surrounded by a rampart which was replaced two centuries later by a Cyclopean wall which was also a sacred enclosure and a divine sanctuary.

We follow the Ancient Way of the Panathenians and come first of all to the Beulé Gate which owes its name to the archaeologist who brought it to light in 1853 from beneath a Turkish buttress which supported a Roman stairway constructed towards the end of the 2nd century. Flanked by two towers, or rather by pylons of irregular shape, it opens on to the axis of the Propylaeum. It dates from the Byzantine era and is pyramidal in form. Beyond it, two lateral staircases of the Roman era lead to two small terraces, formerly with porticoes, which were used by the guards.

We go towards the PROPYLAEA leaving the substructure of the Temple of Wingless Victory to the right and, to the left on a platform, the pedestal of the monument to Agrippa in Hymettus marble, doubtless set up in the 2nd century B.C. to take the statue of an Athenean benefactor which was later replaced by that of another patron of the arts, Vipsanius Agrippa, son-in-law of Augustus. The Propylaea, of Pentelic marble, form a majestic monumental entrance which inspired the admiration of the Ancients. Composed of a central body framed by two recessed wings, they were constructed under Pericles by the architect Mnesicles on the site of the Propylaeum of Pisistratus of the 6th century B.C. This occupied the site of the former main gateway to the Mycenaean citadel. In the 17th century the explosion in the powder magazine which the Turks had installed in the central vestibule greatly damaged the building.

The central section is divided by a transversal wall with five doors closed by heavy wooden shutters. The Sacred Way used to pass through the central door and this was followed by the Panathenean processions and the animals chosen for the sacrifice.

The wings are composed of a portico with Doric columns and corner pillars. The northern one, which is the best preserved, used to house the Pinacotheque. It consisted of a vestibule and three Doric columns *in antis* and a rectangular hall where the paintings were displayed, separated from the vestibule by a wall and two asymmetrical windows flanked by pilasters whose capitals still keep traces of their polychrome decoration.

The southern wing, much smaller than the other, has only one room, and from here we can reach the platform of the TEMPLE OF ATHENA NIKE commonly called the Wingless Victory. It was built by Callicrates in Pentelic marble on a podium with three steps and inaugurated in 421. It has a *cella* which used to shelter the statue of the cult. This was a reproduction of a very ancient wooden *xoanon*, destroyed by the Persians during the sack of the Acropolis when the old sanctuary was also destroyed.

On the entablature above the Ionic columns and on the other three sides, a continuous frieze of reliefs has been almost completely replaced. Casts occupy the spaces of those taken to London by Lord Elgin. Unfortunately all of them are damaged and the heads have disappeared as well as all the details. Nevertheless one can make out the *Assembly of Olympus* with Zeus and Poseidon flanking Athena, whilst on the other surfaces, battle scenes between Greek, Persians and Boeotians are depicted.

Other bas-reliefs used to decorate the parapet which surmounted the cornice, fragments of which have been found and are displayed in the Acropolis Museum. They represented winged victories preparing the ritual victim for sacrifice to Athena.

A useful peep-hole in the floor makes it possible to distinguish on the paving of the *cella*, the remains of the archaic temple of the 6th century and of a staircase leading down to a subterranean room.

Between the graceful temple of Athena Nike and the majestic colonnade of the Parthenon, there used to be a number of other monuments of which there only remain the bases or fragments. First there was the *Brauronion* or the Temenos of Artemis Brauronia, the Bear Goddess whose cult brought from the Deme of Brauron was celebrated by maidens and women. It was built in the time of Cimon, then refashioned when the Propylaea of Mnesicles were constructed. We can make out a wall cut out of the rock which was formerly surmounted by dressed blocks of limestone. At the foot of the wall, cavities were cut to take the *stele* and there are some steps carved into the rock indicating the entrance to the sanctuary.

Opposite, a dozen metres to the left of the Sacred Way, there used to be a bronze quadriga consecrated by the Athenians after their victory of 505 B.C. over the Boeotians and the Chalcidians. Then came the celebrated Athena Promachos, the colossal bronze statue, more than 9 metres high, which was the work of Phidias. In the reign of Justinian, it was taken to Byzantium, but in A.D. 1203 it was broken up by the populace because the outstretched hands of the goddess reminded them of their western invaders.

We then skirt an esplanade which was doubtless the *enceinte* of Athena Ergana (Athena the Artisan) where workmen and their wives laid down contributions offered out of their wages.

Further on, was the Chalcotheque or depot of weapons and the spurs of ships, of which the goddess was the protectress. This building was composed of a rectangular gallery preceded by a portico.

We have now arrived before the PARTHENON, raised up to the glory of Athena which remains the most impressive and the most perfect monument of Greek civilization. It was built between 447 B.C. and 432 B.C. under the inspiration of Pericles with Phidias as Master of Works and Ictinos as architect. The fragments of the decoration of the earlier temple, the necatompedon, have been discovered among the mounds of earth of the re-assembled terrace to the south. The Parthenon remained intact until the fall of the Roman Empire and was constantly enriched by new gifts. It was damaged in the 6th century when it was transformed into a Christian church and, after the edict of A.D. 426 of Theodosius II, the statue of Athena Parthenos by Phidias was carried off to Byzantium.

In A.D. 1460 the church was converted into a mosque, and a minaret was set up in the south-west corner of the *opisthodome*. In 1687, during the siege commanded by Koenigsmark, a shell blew up the monument which had been used as a powder magazine by the Turks. In 1787 the Count of Choiseul-Goussier took back to France a fragment of the frieze and two *metopes* picked up in the debris. Lord Elgin sent to the British Museum a dozen statues, 56 slabs of the frieze, 15 metopes and some marbles from the Erechtheum and the temple of Athena Nike.

The Parthenon is a Doric temple built in Pentelic marble on a foundation of limestone with 8 columns on the façades and 17 along the side (counting the angle columns as 2). The columns of the external galleries carried an entablature made up of an architrave, a frieze and a cornice. The frieze, as is the case in all Doric temples, was decorated with triglyphs and carved metopes numbering 92, of which very few are still in place, those that are being the most damaged. They represent combats of the Giants; those of the west a combat of Amazons. Of the southern metopes only one remains which represents a Centaur wrestling with a Greek. It belongs to a series representing the combat of the Lapiths aided by the Greeks. Those to the north depicted scenes from the Trojan War.

The pediments were decorated with marble sculpture, partly the work of Phidias. The eastern pediment showed the Birth of Athena in armour before Zeus; there only remains a few heads and two feet in position, two of the four horses of Helios and one of the horses of Silenus. The greater part of the fragments that we see are copies of the originals, now in the British Museum.

The west pediment depicts the dispute of Athena and of Poseidon, symbolizing the rivalry between Athena and Eleusis for the possession of Attica: the two divinities occupy the centre. They stand separated by the olive tree which had given the victory to Athena. Only two figures are in position on the left. They are thought to represent Cecrops and his daughter Aglaura and make up the most beautiful and most complete piece of sculpture remaining in Athens. At the opposite corner a reclining figure of a woman is perhaps the spring Callirhoe.

The temple, bounded on the long sides by walls, was entered on each face by porticoes of six Doric columns. The galleries were covered with coffered ceilings, decorated with rosettes and leaves. Finally, the various details were brought out by the use of colour, of which only vestiges remain. The background of the metopes must have been red, and of the pediments, blue, and doubtless these Greek temples had an entirely different aspect from what we now see. Our whole idea of Hellenic art would be quite changed if we knew the original appearance of the monuments.

The frieze which surrounded the whole temple beneath the ceiling of the galleries, depicted the procession of the great Panathenians which took place every four years. First there was the preparation for the departure, the horsemen beginning to mount their steeds, then the file of horsemen, the chariots, the sacrificial priests, magistrates, etc., and finally the great company of the gods.

The interior of the temple comprised, beyond the vestibule,

the Hecatompedon which had much in common with the archaic temple. It was divided into three naves by two rows of Doric columns linked at the back by a transversal colonnade of five columns. In the central nave stood the statue to Athena Parthenos, all in gold and ivory, carved by Phidias and 12 metres high—15 counting the base. This was consecrated in 438 B.C. in the presence of Pericles; a priestly family was entrusted with seeing to its maintenance, humidifying the air artificially when it was necessary. We then come to the Parthenon proper, the Hall of the Virgins, which was used as a treasury and whose ceiling was supported by four Doric columns. The *opisthodome*, or black portico, was closed by grilles like the entrance to the vestibule.

We then reach the ACROPOLIS MUSEUM where, among the splendid exhibits, are an unusual pediment of painted tufa, of the end of the 7th century B.C., the Moschophere, an archaic statue of the 6th century, several works attributed to Phaidimos, one of the greatest sculptors of the archaic period, numerous *korai* (statues of maidens), the group of Procis and Itys which Pausanias attributed to Alcemenes, tablets belonging to the frieze of the Parthenon, and fragments of sculpture from the pediment.

We will now continue towards the ERECHTHEUM formed by the juxtaposition of several temples. It enchants us by the elegance of its porticoes and the grace of its caryatids. It is one of the most ethereal and the most delicate Ionic monuments in existence.

The Erechtheum symbolized the origin of the power of Athens. It is there that Athena and Poseidon had put forward their claims for the possession of Attica; Athena offering up the miracle of the olive tree, Poseidon bringing forth a jet of salt water with a blow of his trident. At the same time it was the sanctuary where the more or less legendary heroes, creators of the city, Erechtheus, Cecrops, Pandrosos and Butes, were venerated. This sanctuary combined the cult of Athena with that of Poseidon and the olive tree was venerated as well as the traces of the mark of the trident, the place where Erechtheus was mortally wounded and the tomb of Cecrops.

Nothing remains of the primitive sanctuary in polychrome tufa which was burnt down by the Persians. Its reconstruction in marble, undertaken by Pericles after 421 B.C., recommenced in 409 B.C. under the direction of the architect Philocles, was completed in 406 B.C. It was converted into a church in the 7th century and into a harem by the Turks in A.D. 1463.

The principal building consists of a rectangle, to which are attached three projecting porches. A frieze of blue limestone from Eleusis surrounded the whole edifice with reliefs of figures in white marble of which some fragments have been deposited in the Acropolis Museum.

The *cella* to the east dedicated to Athena Polias, was preceded by a *pronaos* with a portico of six Ionic columns, one of which is in the British Museum. The wall at the back of the vestibule with two windows and an entrance doorway was removed to make room for the apse of the Byzantine church, and the two longitudinal walls date from this conversion. The hall, which had no floor, was divided by a transversal wall into two parts; the first being the *cella* of Athena Polios where there used to stand an ancient idol in olivewood alleged to have fallen from heaven and dedicated to Cecrops, the mythical founder of Athens.

Each year the statue was dressed in a new tunic woven by the Arrhephores and the priestesses of Athena.

A modern stairway replaces the ancient one and gives access to the north portico whose façade is composed of four elegant Ionic columns and one in reverse on each side. It is a marvel of purity and grace with its decorated coffered ceiling, the ornamentation of its door, its frieze and its architrave. It shelters the section of the rock which had kept the marks of Poseidon's trident and which it is possible to see in a little crypt

3. ATHENS : TEMPLE OF WINGLESS VICTORY.

4. ATHENS : ERECHTHEUM.

5. ATHENS : THESEUM.

6. ATHENS: LITTLE METROPOLIS.

through a hole in the floor. Later these marks were attributed to the thunderbolt of Zeus.

At the back of the portico there were two doors, the smaller one opened on to the *pandroseion* and the olive tree of Athena, the larger one on to the *cella* of the Erechtheum. It is surrounded by Ionic decoration of extreme beauty. The Sanctuary of the Erechtheum is situated at a lower level than the *cella* of Athena. It doubtless contained the altars of Hephaestos and of Butes, as well as a crypt of several compartments. First of all was the Hall of the Mouth, so called because the kerbed observation hole in the floor was a sort of pit in which the sea of Erechtheus could be seen flowing under the trident of Poseidon. This hall communicated with the Pandroseion and the Cecropion to the west and, to the south, was the portico of the *korai* with a little stairway of eleven steps.

The western façade, restored after the Roman modification of the 1st century B.C., bounded the Pandroseion or the Sanctuary of Sandros, formed of a court which contains the olive tree of Athena, an altar to Zeus Herkeios and doubtless a chapel of Pandros, daughter of Cecrops. The funerary sanctuary of the mythical king of Athens was to be found in the angle formed by the wall of the façade and the substructure of the ancient temple.

We finally see the Portico of the *Korai*, the most original part of the Erechtheum. On a base of great paving stones stand six statues of young girls dressed in long Ionian tunics, their arms hanging by their sides, their heads bearing a circular capital decorated with ovoids and spearheads on which rests the architrave decorated with discs in relief and with a serrated cornice. The second figure to the west, now in the British Museum, has been replaced by a concrete cast.

The grace of these young girls, with their easy noble carriage is the personification of all the poetry and fascination of the classical art of Attica.

The Portico of the *Korai* partly rests on the foundation of the former temple to Athena whose ruins are spread over the terrace to the south. We can see there, protected by grilles, two bases for columns of wood similar to those of the Mycenaean palaces of Tiryns and of Mycenae.

We then find the ruins of a square building of the 5th century B.C., which was the dwelling place of virgins, daughters of noble birth, aged between 7 and 11 years, entrusted to help with the rites of the goddess.

We go back to the Propylaea and then climb up to the summit of the hill of Areopagus, consecrated to Ares, and to the Erinyes whose sanctuary is not far from the Acropolis of the Eupatries and which originally served as an asylum for murderers. The senate of the Areopagus was held here and was invested with the control of the constitution and its customs. The deserters of Cheronea, Demosthenes and the courtesan Phryne, the model of Praxiteles, were judged before this Senate.

A flight of 16 steps leads to a little platform cut in the rock bordered by triple tiers of rock, forming the three sides of a sort of exedra open to the south. Above, a terrace adjoins an isolated cube of rock which could be the altar to Athena Areia, or one of the two stones which serve as seats for the parties concerned, the Stone of the Outrage for the accused and the Stone of Resentment for the accuser.

From the Areopagus there is a superb view of the *agora* but before going there, we can visit the Museum and the Pnyx.

We will point out first of all, between the hill of the Pnyx and the Areopagus, excavations which have brought to light the remains of a whole quarter of the Deme of Melitus flanking a road which started from the Agora and is 250 metres long and 4 wide.

We can see on the other side of the avenue Apostolou Pavlou, a fountain of the 6th century which may be the celebrated fountain of Callirhoe, called also the fountain of Enneacrounes (with nine mouths).

To the right of the road, lies the Amynsion, sanctuary of the warrior-hero Amynos, an auxiliary of Asclepios, and 30 metres further on, before reaching a little triangular island surrounded by a polygonal wall in limestone from the Acropolis, we find the DIONYSION EN LIMNAIS (of the marshes) which may be the most ancient sanctuary of Dionysus in Athens. On this sanctuary and on the adjacent street, the Dionysiac fraternity of the Iabacchoi superimposed their place of reunion, the Baccheion, in the 2nd century A.D.

On the other side of the road are boundary stones with inscriptions which used to limit the façade of a kind of club whose site stretched out to the west under the pavement.

The summit of the Hill of the Muses, formerly called the MOUSEION, is crowned with a monumental tomb known as the Monument of Philopappos, erected by the Athenians between A.D. 114 and 116 in honour of a Syrian prince, a Roman dignitary, a citizen and benefactor of Athens, Caïus Julius Antiochos Philopappos, of the dynasty of the Commagenes.

The upper part had three niches which, apart from the statue of Philopappos which can be seen in the central one, held statues of his ancestors : to the left, his grandfather Antiochus IV, the last King of the Commagenes dethroned by Vespasian and, to the right, Seleucos I Nicator, founder of the dynasty.

We can see also, 50 metres to the north, the remains of a tower of the fortress of Demetrios Poliocetes and notice that there was in the 5th century an entire rupestral village which stretched across the slopes separating the hills of the Museion from the Pnyx and over the sides of the Areopagus. These quarters were in the interior of the *enceinte* of Themistocles and of the Long Walls. Although overpopulated during the Peloponnesian War, they were deserted in the following century.

We now descend as far as the little chapel of *Haghios*

Dimitrios Lombardaris which still has some Byzantine paintings. It stands near the Tourist Pavilion and not far from the troglodyte dwelling falsely called the prison of Socrates and of another troglodyte dwelling known as the Tomb of Cimon consisting of a cave entered through a courtyard carved out of the rock.

We then come upon the entrance to the PNYX, the meeting place of the People's Assembly, where the great orators of Athens used to discourse in the 4th century B.C.: Aristides, Themistocles, Pericles, Demosthenes.

The Pnyx is a great terrace which stretches at the foot of a little cliff where the audience collected. The orators stood upon a projecting cube of rock.

On the cliff face a large alcove and other smaller ones formed part of a Roman sanctuary dedicated to Zeus Hypsistos and, behind the tribune, foundations cut in the rock might have been the site of the altar to Zeus Agoraios where the archons came to take the oath.

Further on, there are several other foundations cut into the rock even though there remains practically nothing of the two porticoes erected on the summit of the hill.

We will now proceed to the excavations of the Agora and begin our visit with the THESEUM, so called because most of the sculpture deals with the exploits of Theseus. It is in actual fact a sanctuary dedicated to Vulcan (Hephaestos).

This Doric temple which contains several Ionic elements was constructed between 449 and 444 B.C. and is therefore more ancient than the Parthenon. It is the best-preserved of all the Greek temples and it stands out on its rocky eminence with distinction and a noble power.

Hephaestos was the god of blacksmiths and potters of which there were many in the district and the temple was surrounded by a garden with vines, myrtles and pomegranates planted in pots and watered by a system of canals.

It is a peripteral hexastyle temple whose façade, turned

towards the Agora, leads to a *pronaos* and a *cella* which has a Doric colonnade of two superimposed orders of four columns to the west and seven columns on the two long sides. It contained the bronze statue of Hephaestos and of Athena Hephaestia, protectors of the artisans of the ceramic quarter.

The mouldings of the peristyle of the *pronaos* still have the remains of painted decoration in the form of palmettes and meanders. The ceiling, whose twenty coffers are decorated with painted stars, which also appear on the soffits, is in a good state of preservation. In contrast, the carvings which used to decorate the temple are for the most part either destroyed or in a very bad state. Those of the pediments have disappeared with the exception of a few fragments now displayed in the Agora Museum. Only the ten metopes of the east and four of the north and south sides are decorated. The walls of the *secos* under the peristyle to the east on the side of the *pronaos*, and to the west on the side of the *opisthodome*, are decorated along the entablature with two continuous friezes.

At the beginning of the 5th century A.D., the temple was converted into a church dedicated to St. George and it was then that a door was cut making it possible to go into the *cella* in the *opisthodome*. The sculptured frieze to be seen beneath the gallery depicts the battles of the Lapiths assisted by the Athenians against the Centaurs during the celebrations of the marriage of Pirithoos, friend of Theseus, who can be seen in the centre of the right hand group armed with a large round shield. In the left hand group Pirithoos brings help to Kaeneus threatened by two Centaurs armed with a lump of rock.

The decorated *metopes* to the east deal with the exploits of Hercules, whilst those of Theseus feature on the *metopes* of the north and south. We can see Hercules and the Nemean lion, Hercules and Ioalos fighting the Hydra of Lerna, capturing the Arcadian stag, carrying off Cerberus, Hercules with the Queen of the Amazons, with Eurytion, with Geryones and Hercules receiving the apples of the Hesperides.

As for Theseus, we see him as Conqueror of Procrustes, victor in the wrestling with Merkyon, and with Skiron, Theseus killing the wild sow of Krommyon, Theseus with the Minotaur, with the bull of Marathon, with the brigand Periphetes and the brigand Sinis.

The frieze of the *pronaos*, which is badly mutilated, shows a combat going on in the presence of six seated divinities.

The AGORA, which we shall now visit, was the meeting place of the Athenian people who came here to discuss subjects of public interest. A law forbade anyone who had been guilty of crime or whose conduct was reprehensible from being present. This place was the heart and soul of the city. It was here that the public services were established, it was here that business was carried on. The Acropolis was the sacred dwelling of the gods, but the *Agora* was the civic centre where the great affairs of the city were discussed.

It was a huge square bordered with porticoes and public buildings, decorated with statues and ex-votos and fountains shaded by great trees. The principal streets of the town met here and distances were calculated from the Altar of the Twelve Gods which stood almost in the centre.

The main official buildings were in the south-west corner: the Senate, the Tholos, the Metroon. Political meetings were also held here, particularly voting on ostracism.

Following the destruction caused by the Persians, several buildings had to be reconstructed and great changes took place during the Hellenistic period. The sacking of the city by Sulla in 86 B.C. damaged many edifices and the invasion of the Goths in A.D. 267 ruined many more. Towards A.D. 400 most of the buildings were reconstructed.

First we see the foundations of the Tholos, a circular construction erected towards 470 B.C. Here sat the Senators or *Prytanes* numbering fifty. In the Hellenistic period it was preceded by an outside portico whose first step can still be seen.

Then we come to the foundations of a number of buildings in the *Bouleuterion*, or Senate, and the *Metroon*, the Temple of the Mother of The Gods.

The Senate, whose ruins are visible at the foot of the slope of the *Agora*, was erected at the end of the 5th century B.C. next to an even older edifice whose foundations still subsist.

The *Metroon*, situated on a slightly lower level, was composed of four rooms opening under a portico and has only the foundations and some portions of the walls, which, with the substructure, are later than the conglomeration of stones whose origins are too complex for the layman. It was built in its latest form at the end of the 2nd century B.C. and it served as a depot for the state archives which were recorded on papyrus, parchment or tablets of marble. The central part, surrounded by an interior colonnade, was open to the sky. We can still see the greater part of the stylobate of the peristyle. In the 5th century A.D. the floor of this room was covered with mosaics decorated with geometric and floral motifs.

After having crossed the Great Drain which drew off the rainwater from the hills towards Eridanos, we go to the centre of the *Agora* to see the enclosure of Heros Eponymes. We can make out vestiges of the limestone posts linked by horizontal stones which surrounded the pedestal, where stood the statues of ten legendary heroes of Attica; at either end was a bronze tripod. Doubtless constructed in the last quarter of the 5th century B.C., it served as a place for tablets on which were engraved laws, regulations and eulogies for everyone to see.

When, in 508 B.C., Cleisthenes began his administrative reforms, he gave to each of the ten tribes which made up the population of Attica the name of one of the ten heroes who then became the patron protector of the tribe. The number of tribes was increased to twelve in 307 B.C. and to thirteen under Hadrian.

A little further on, continuing towards the *Agora*, the

remains of a great altar in Pentelic marble date from the end of the 4th century B.C. It may be the altar to Zeus Agoraios where the archons came to take the oath on assuming office. It was originally on the Pnyx.

There still remain the marble steps, the great central body of blocks of poros and some details of the superstructure.

Then, on the other side of the enclosure of Eponymous Heroes, stands the base of a monument raised up in honour of Quintus Trebellius Rufus of Toulouse, benefactor and *archon* of Athens in about A.D. 90.

We now see a statue of Hadrian in Pentelic marble found near the *Metroon*. Between the wall of this building and the Temple of Apollo a broad passage with a monumental stairway leads directly to the Hephaesteum.

The *Temple of Apollo* (Apollo Patroos) was constructed in its final state towards the end of the 4th century of our era. Patroos was the father of Ion, mythical ancestor of the Ionians, of whom the Athenians considered themselves the descendants. The temple may have contained a gigantic statue of Apollo now in the Agora Museum and which is said to be the work of Euphranor.

An earlier archaic temple of the first quarter of the 6th century had been destroyed by the Persians and was replaced by a second towards the middle of the 4th century B.C., consecrated to Zeus Phratios and Athena Phratia; the foundations to the north are still visible. The portico in front of the *cella* was added during the 2nd century B.C.

Hardly anything remains of the celebrated stoa of Zeus Eleuthereus, also called the stoa of Basileios. This royal portico was a continuation of Apollo Patroos built towards 430 or 421 B.C. after the Peace of Nicias. It was the seat of the tribunal of the archon-king who was elected each year and it was also the place where trials of impiety and homicide, the threats to the security of the state, were judged by the tribunal of Areopagus and examined by the Court of Ostracism. It was

7. ATHENS : MONASTERY OF KAISARIANI.

8. ATHENS: THEATRE OF DIONYSOS.

the most populous place of the *Agora* and it was here that Socrates and his friends discussed philosophical questions.

In front of the stoa of Zeus there used to be a number of monuments of which only the foundations remain, notably a round base on which there used to be a statue perhaps of Zeus Eleuthereus, and an altar.

More to the east, the Altar of the Twelve Gods, consecrated towards the end of the 6th century B.C. by the Pisistradides, was situated near the junction of the Panathenian Way and other roads.

To the south of the Altar of the Twelve Gods, a rising in the ground indicates the site of the Temple of Ares built about 440 or 436 B.C. on the site of the Roman Agora and removed stone by stone to the Greek Agora towards the end of the 1st century B.C. under Augustus. Pausanius saw the statue of the cult executed by Alcamenes and, in the surrounding area, a number of statues attributed to famous sculptors such as the group of the Tyrannoctones. It was a Doric temple rather like the Theseum and was doubtless destroyed during the invasion of the Heruls in A.D. 267. The ruins were used to construct the Wall of Valerian ten years later.

We now find the three colossal statues of two tritons and a giant, each standing on a massive pedestal. They used to be part of the gymnasium built in the 5th century A.D. on the site of the Odeon of Agrippa built in about the year 15 B.C. by Agrippa, minister to Augustus. The ruins can be found to the south. As well as the stage and the orchestra we can make out some of the tiers of the hemicycle. The statues of giants which were used, later on, in the construction of the gymnasium had originally been carved to decorate the northern façade of the Odeon.

Behind the Odeon stood the Middle Stoa built in the 2nd century B.C. and 150 metres long. Blocks of stone to the right indicate that there was a Roman Temple here and, at the end, are the ruins of offices and booths among which was perhaps the one belonging to the cobbler Simon with whom Socrates used to talk at such length.

Near the buildings, the Great Drain branches off into a secondary canal which flows under the stoa. A 6th-century boundary stone bears the inscription: "I am the boundary of the *Agora.*"

We then reach the ruins of the *Heliaia*, the People's Tribunal, an institution whose origins go back to the 6th century, the time of Solon. In those days the people assembled in the open air at sunrise, which accounts for the name. Against the wall to the south are the remains of a water clock of the 4th century B.C. with a little rectangular basin, a stairway and a well. There was also a fountain and a basin of sacred water for symbolical purification before entering into the *Agora.*

A long portico built before the middle of the 2nd century B.C. limited the southern end of the *Agora* between the Heliaia and the Panathenian Way. It replaced a portico of the last quarter of the 5th century B.C.

THE CHURCH OF THE HOLY APOSTLES was founded in the 11th century upon the ruins of a semicircular fountain of the 2nd century A.D. The church has been remodelled and restored many times, but still preserves the decoration of its exterior and some beautiful Byzantine frescoes.

Behind the churches we can make out the ruins of a fountain of the 6th century B.C. and those of the Argyrokopeion, or the mint, where the beautiful Athenian coins displayed in the Agora Museum were made.

The Panathenian Way, which we still see here paved with great blocks laid down in the Roman era, is flanked by the remains of the so-called Wall of Valerian.

The Portico of Attalus was reconstructed by the American School and its over-brilliant whiteness is somewhat offensive in this area of mellow ruins. Originally built in the 2nd century B.C. by Attalus II, King of Pergamum, it now houses the Agora Museum which contains fragments of architecture, sculpture and ceramics unearthed in the excavation of the *Agora*. This stoa is composed of two superimposed colonnades, Doric below, Ionic above, making 134 columns in all.

We leave the Agora to proceed to the CERAMIC CEMETERY which also has a small museum. We reach it by way of the Sacred Gate and the Dipylon and follow the path which goes to the right towards the ruins. First we come across vestiges of the *enceinte* of Athens constructed by Themistocles, remodelled by Conon and lined with a wall by Lycurgus. It still has a frontage of 200 metres with two gateways, the Sacred Gate and the Dipylon Gate. Behind the Wall of Lycurgus the polygonal foundation stones of the Wall of Themistocles can be seen.

We now reach the Sacred Way which skirts the Eridanos and arrive at the Sacred Gate whose masonry is of several different periods. A passage which is 32 metres long and 12 metres wide is enclosed between lateral walls and defended by two corner towers of which one, to the north, is partly Roman and divided in two by the bank of the Eridanos.

To reach the Dipylon we skirt the *enceinte*, constructed in the time of Conon, which separates the two gates. It was defended by two projecting square towers. On the inner side, the space between the two gates was occupied by the substructures, the Pompeion, the store for the properties used during the processions and at the point of departure of the Panathenian cortège. It dates partly from the time of Hadrian and replaces a Greek edifice of the 4th century B.C.

The DIPYLON, or Dipylon Gate, at the entrance to the Academia Road is formed of twin gates built between 338 and 326 under Lycurgus at the same time as the doubling of the wall. The outer gate, cut in the rampart, was flanked with two square towers, one of which has disappeared, and it consisted of two entrances separated by a pilaster, against which stands the marble base of a votive monument surrounded by a bench.

Passing through the outer gate, we reach a space situated between two ramparts so that the enemy who had managed to penetrate thus far was trapped under the fire of the defenders, as was the case in 200 B.C. with the soldiers of Philip V of Macedonia. In times of peace the traveller who arrived in Athens was welcomed here by the Athenian courtesans and invited to go and sleep with them.

The lower gate, framed by two great square towers reinforced by salients, also had two entrances 3·45 metres wide which allowed the passage of two chariots. Near the central pier a round altar is dedicated to Zeus Herkeios, Hermes and Akemas.

From the inner gate of the Dipylon we can reach the propylon, or the entrance to the Pompeion, of the beginning of the 4th century B.C. Then, by following the traces of the ancient Academia road, we find the very ancient sarcophagus of Philotera, and to the left a number of tombs partly exposed which belonged to the Cemetery of the Great Ceramic famous for the beauty of its tombs and notably those of Selon, of Thrasibules and of Pericles, all monuments set up at the expense of the state. This cemetery was also famous for its funeral orations spoken by such great Athenian orators as Pericles, Lysias, Demosthenes and Hyperides on the occasion of Epitaphia and national funerals.

This necropolis occupied the ancient suburb of the Outer Ceramic where there were many potters and tile makers. From the 7th century B.C. the dead were interred outside the ramparts along the roads. This made them easily accessible and facilitated the cult of ancestor worship, at the same time allowing passers-by to admire these exceptionally sumptuous tombs and to perpetuate the cult of the illustrious dead.

Several funerary monuments to Lacedemonian officers who helped to overthrow the Thirty Tyrants in 403 B.C. have been found.

Do not miss, at the point where the Academy Road meets

the modern road to Piraeus, the remains of the circular baths built after the Persian invasion of 480.

Retracing our steps we follow the Sacred Way which takes us to the most important group of tombs. A hundred metres from the Sacred Gate we can enter the Pathway of the Tombs which links the Sacred Way with the Piraeus Road. At the corner formed by the two ways there rises up the little sanctuary of the Tritopatores, or ancestors, of the 5th century B.C. The most ancient tombs dating from the 7th century are found in this area and are formed of quite deep ditches or wells containing only one skeleton or the ashes of a single person with the funerary offerings left in the trenches lined with sun-dried bricks.

The Pathway of the Tombs is bordered by concessions belonging to rich Athenian families and to foreigners of the 4th century. Each enclosure contained several tombs of a variety of types. There are little chapels ornamented with pediments, sculptures, *stele* with palm decorations, or quadrangular tablets: there are sarcophagi of painted brick, *loutrophori* or *lecythes*, and simple *cippi*. The most luxurious of these tombs were constructed before the law of Demetrios of Phalerus who insisted on much simpler designs in 317 B.C.

Beyond the enclosure dedicated to ancestors, we can see slabs and *stele* bearing the names of Philocrates, of Phanocles and of Hipparete the grand-daughter of Alcibiades whose tumulus stone in the form of an altar must have been placed here about 350 B.C.

A little off the pathway, the Tomb of Eucoline is ornamented with a bas-relief depicting the deceased holding a bird: he has a dog at his feet and is surrounded by two women and a man of his family. More to the west, the monument of Aristion is decorated with a relief where Death holds a bird in his hand: he stands in front of his servant and above a Syren in the attitude of a weeper.

Several metres further on, on the edge of the pathway,

stands the *stele* of Menes on horseback and also a *stele* of Samakion.

The most interesting funerary monuments are to be found on the north side in the concession of Korobibus of Melitus, the *stele* of Korobibos and a reproduction of the *stele* of Hegeso; the original is in the National Museum.

The last concession on the eastern side belonged to Eubios of Potamos and contains the *stele* of Euphrosyne constructed about 386 B.C. as well as the Column of Bion and the base of a *stele*.

Returning to the fork of the Pathway of the Tombs and the Sacred Way, we can see the enclosure of Nikostrate and Kephisodoros with three slabs, the concession of Lysimachides of Acharnes with a bas-relief of Charon, an *ex-voto* depicting the funerary feast of two couples in Hades of the Roman era and a mastiff and a lion in Hymettus marble.

On the upper terraces, the Temenos of Hecate has a beautiful bas-relief of Hydrophoria, whilst to the left is a votif relief embedded in a square altar, a dedication to Artemis and a home altar with an *omphalos* in the middle and a niche of brick containing the triangular base of a statue of the triple Hecate. Further to the south are some sarcophagi, including one to Daphnos in rough brick with a coat of paint and some *cippi*.

On leaving we can visit a little museum where the most valuable fragments found in the cemetery are displayed.

We return to the city by way of Ermou and Assomaton square, where the *Church of SS. Assomates* dates from the 11th century.

ITINERARY II

ATHENS II

Plaka — Monument to Lysicrates — Tower of the Winds — Roman Agora — Hadrian's Library — Church of SS. Theodores — Little Metropolis.

THIS second itinerary deals with the old quarter of Athens where little Byzantine churches can be found in tortuous lanes standing next to ancient ruins. It has kept a picturesque charm which everyone must appreciate; and it is most enjoyable to stroll about here or to sit down in the small popular restaurants which serve such local dishes as grilled fish or roast lamb.

The PLAKA is the oldest quarter of Athens and even if it has nothing in common with its character at the time of Pericles at least it has kept a great deal of the atmosphere of the last century.

We will begin by taking a swift look at several little Byzantine churches. First of all, the *Church of Haghios Nicodemos* in Philhellinon Street, which is sometimes called *Soteira tou Likodimou* and may have been founded in the first quarter of the 11th century, but it was partly demolished in 1780. Beneath the church and the garden, crypts contain several tombs, including one of the founder, and also some Roman baths and cisterns of the time of Hadrian. By way of Kidathieon Street we arrive at the *Church of Soteira tou Kotaki* which dates from the 13th century and is designed on the plan of a Greek cross with a dome, but which has been transformed into a basilica with three naves.

We then go via Farmaki Street to the *Church of Haghia Ekaterini*, surrounded by a courtyard which dates from the 13th century, but which was remodelled later. The apses and the dome were not changed. On a lower level can be seen two columns with a fragment of an architrave which belonged either to a temple of Artemis or to some baths.

Lysicrates Street leads to a little garden where the MONUMENT TO LYSICRATES stands. It is a single marble rotunda constructed for a bronze tripod given as a prize to the Lysicrates Choregus, in 335 B.C. In Ancient Greece the Choregus kept, at their own expense, a choir and dancers to give theatrical performances. Those which Lysicrates patronized had received a tripod for their victory in the Dionysian festival games. Other monuments built along this street of the Tripods, which adjoins the Theatre of Dionysos, have disappeared but this one has been preserved because the French Capucin monks bought the land in 1669 and incorporated the Lysicrates monument in their monastery. It is a pseudo-peripteral *tholos* and the *cella* is decorated with six columns with Corinthian capitals and friezes of tripods in relief.

It is surmounted by an architrave of three bands with, above the inscription, a frieze representing Dionysos, seated on a rock, caressing a panther. He is surrounded by young satyrs who serve him with wine from two goblets. Other satyrs, armed with thyrses, torches and clubs, pursue Tyrrhaenian pirates who leap into the sea and are already half changed into dolphins. On the ridge of the conical roof made of a single slab of marble and decorated with imitation tiles and consols, terminated by acanthus leaves, stands the tripod won by Lysicrates.

Near here at the entrance to Epimenedou stands the 1st-century *Basilica of Haghios Demetrios*. We now take Shelley Street and Epimarkou, and come to a square where we shall find another church, *Haghios Nicolaos tou Rengava*, founded in the 11th century but re-modelled later. This was part of the Palace of the Rengave family which produced a number of Byzantine emperors and patriarchs.

We can then see the minute church of *Haghios Georgios tou Vrouchou* partly constructed on the rock of the Acropolis. The single nave is barrel vaulted and probably of Frankish origin.

Going down by the stairway of Erechtheos Street, we pass the entrance to the Metochi tou Panaghiou Tafou monastery on the right. This is a dependency of the Holy Sepulchre of Jerusalem. Its church, *Haghii Anargyri*, dates from the 17th century but has been very much restored. The iconostasis, the throne and the altarpiece of carved and gilded wood, are in the eastern Baroque style.

Behind the church the House of the Exarcate built in 1838 is characteristic of the architecture of the period.

We shall find a charming little church at the corner of Erechtheos and Erotocritou Street, *Haghios Yanis Theologos*, which goes back to the 13th century. Taking Erotocritou and Clepsydras Street which climbs up towards the Acropolis, we find the house of Cleanthis at No. 5 Thoulou Street. It was converted into a *taverna* and at the end of the War of Independence the first university of Athens was installed here.

The first road to the left leads to Aretousas Street in the Anaphiotika quarter where the houses date from the beginning of the 19th century, and the delightful little 14th-century *Church of Metamorphosis* has a grotto converted into a chapel dedicated to Haghia Paraskevi where the altar is made of a beautiful proto-Christian capital. Some traces of painting still remain in the apse and, on a little iconostasis, is an ikon, la Panachia Tricheroussa.

We then take Panos Street and the Rue de Pan to reach the excavations of the Roman Agora and we shall see the graceful TOWER OF THE WINDS, the hydraulic clock of Andronikos built in the 1st century B.C., probably under

Caesar, at the time of a reconstruction of the market. Built of white marble, it contains mechanisms which regulate the flow of water into a cylinder and thus shows the hours according to successive levels. It was called the tomb of Socrates in the Middle Ages. Each of the faces are orientated towards the eight points of the Athenian horizon to which corresponded the winds whose names are engraved along with the symbolical figures carved on the frieze. Boreas is represented as a bearded man who is learning to blow on a conch shell; Kaikias also bearded, empties his shield full of hailstones; Apeliotes appears as a young man bearing fruit and ears of corn; Euros is bearded and wrapped in a mantle; Notos, the wind bringing rain, is represented by a beardless man emptying an urn; Lyps holds part of a ship; Zephyr is symbolized by a young man with a flowing robe from which flowers are scattered; Skiron holds a vase. A sundial is depicted on each face.

We now cross the great court of the ROMAN AGORA which has kept its marble paving in certain places.

In the first half of the 2nd century A.D., the central court was surrounded with porticoes whose smooth columns in Hymettus marble rested on bases of Pentelic marble. To the south and to the east the gallery was occupied by booths. In the south gallery, which is the best preserved, there is a marble fountain.

The west gate of the *Agora*, also called the Gate of Athena Archgetis, was constructed, as the dedication of the architrave tells us, by the Athenian people under the archon Nicias between the year 11 and 12 B.C. Four columns surmounted by a pediment are still standing. An inscription cut in the door jamb of the main door of the *propylaeum* concerns a law of Hadrian which established the amount of oil that producers must reserve for the state.

The *propylaeum* consisted of an outer porch with four Doric columns bearing an entablature and a pediment surmounted by ornaments; the topmost one supported a statue of Lucius Caesar, son of Germanicus adopted by Augustus.

At the edge of the excavations of the Roman Agora, the Fethye Djamila, the Mosque of the Victory, which the Greeks called the Mosque of the Corn Market, is used to display copies of frescoes and mosaics from Byzantine buildings in Greece.

Opposite the Tower of the Winds, in Eolou Street on the right, we find the beautiful carved doorway of an old Moslem School of Theology built by the Turks in 1721.

We then arrive at HADRIAN'S LIBRARY whose most important remains are to be found in Areos Street. Two *exedra* decorate the north and south sides of porticoes surrounding the central court. A pavilion was built on the remains of a basin and was converted into a church, probably at the beginning of the 5th century, by Empress Eudoxia Athenais, wife of Theodosius II.

We go down Pandrosou Street to the main façade of the library, of which there only remains a section preceded by a colonnade. A Byzantine domed church dedicated to the Taxiarques Incorporates was built against the façade in the 10th or 11th century. Some of the frescoes dating from the restoration of 1576 are still visible beneath a protecting roof on the façade of the library.

At the corner of Areos Street, the *Mosque of Dzami tou Pazarou* (the Mosque of the Bazaar) was built in 1759 and has been converted into a museum of the decorative arts.

We must not neglect the popular and picturesque side of this quarter where there are so many booths where every kind of hand-made apparel can be bought from the local craftsmen; purses and bags of coloured leather, embroidery, shoes with pompoms etc. Here if you wish, you can buy everything you need to disguise yourself as an Evzone.

We then come to the *Church of Panaghia of the Great Monastery* which used to be a dependence of the monastery founded in the 10th century, but since it has been very much restored, the structure is of no interest.

By way of Athinas Street, a broad highway which crosses the central market of Athens, then via Evripou Street, we can see the most interesting of all the Athens churches, HAGHIA THEODORI, the Church of SS. Theodores which, according to an inscription above the south door, must have been reconstructed in its present form in about 1070 by Nicolas Calamos on the site of a 5th-century building. Each of the façades has a beautiful little door and the windows are also very finely carved. It is a church on the plan of a Greek Cross with a narthex and surmounted by a dome. The walls of alternating layers of brick and stone are decorated externally with a terracotta frieze with kouphic characters.

The pulpit and the iconostasis are of marble and, 1·5 metres below the present pavement, the pavement of the original church has been found.

By way of Scouleniou, Chrysospilotisa, Haghiou Marcou and Kalamiotu Streets we can reach the *Kapnikarea Church* which is in Ermou Street. Built at the end of the 11th century and also known as the Vasilopoula (daughter of the King) it is, with the Little Metropolis, one of the most remarkable churches in Athens.

The original church on a cruciform plan with a dome was completed later by a lateral nave to the north which was dedicated to St. Barbe. The two naves were linked in the 12th century by a narthex whose four arches surmounted by gables were later pierced by windows which we see today. The beautiful porch with two little columns which leads into the porch with engaged columns and the finely decorated and carved marble lintel date from this period.

We now proceed to the Mitropoleos Square where we shall find the New Cathedral of Athens built in 1840 and the LITTLE METROPOLIS, the most delightful church of Byzantine Athens.

This tiny church, which some date from the beginning of the 11th century and some from the 12th century and which once belonged to the Monastery of St. Nicholas, is not on the same scale as the modern flats which surround it, although its proportions were compatible with the modest houses of Byzantine Athens.

Numerous sculptured antique and Byzantine tablets of stone decorate the outside. On the façade we can see a lintel with two lions facing each other with a cross between them, some Byzantine bas-reliefs depicting symbolic animals, Corinthian capitals and an antique frieze from a monument of the 4th century B.C. representing a liturgical calendar. The months are represented by the signs of the Zodiac with scenes illustrating the principal festivals of each month: the Vintage, dancing, cock fighting, naked athletes, the sacrifice of a bull, and the Great Panathenaea with the prow of a ship mounted on wheels. The coats of arms of the La Roche and Villehardouin families are also displayed.

On the apses there are several inscriptions, antique and Byzantine *stele* and an Archaic bas-relief with dancing girls. On the south side there are various architectural fragments from ancient friezes with triglyphs and metopes and Byzantine *stele*.

Finally on the north side, there are antique *stele* and a *stele* ornamented with vases and shields.

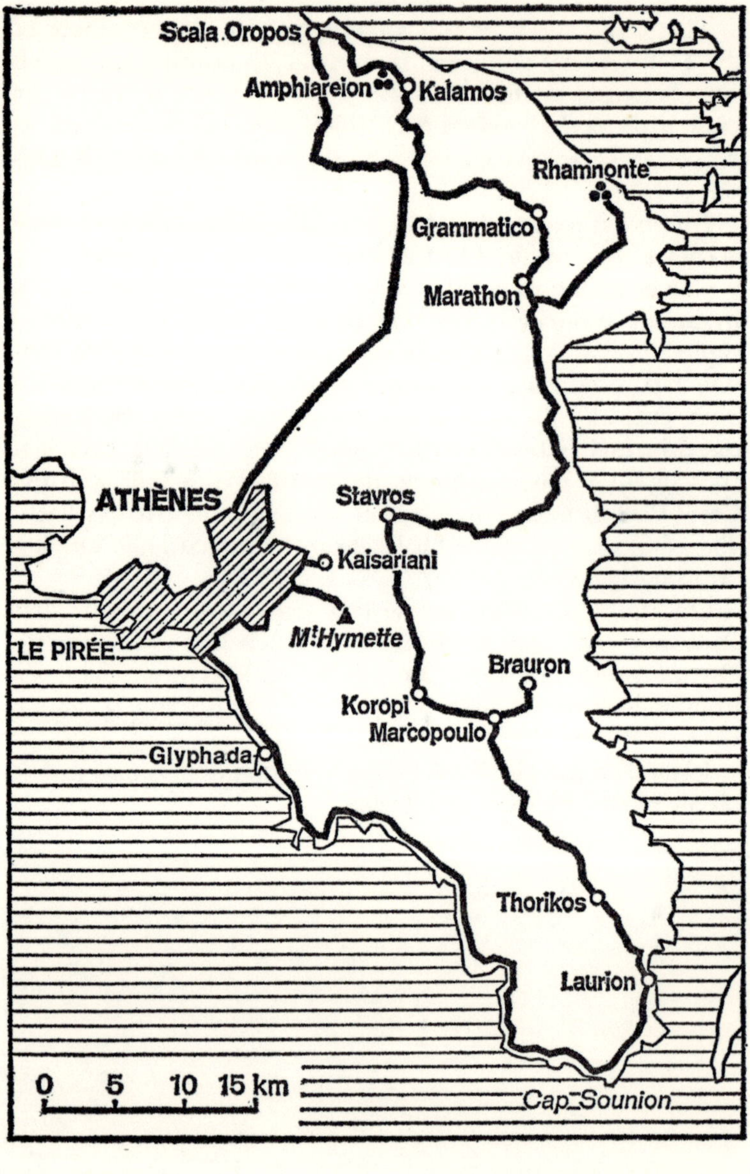
Scala Oropos
Amphiareion
Kalamos
Rhamnonte
Grammatico
Marathon
ATHÈNES
Stavros
Kaisariani
Mt Hymette
LE PIRÉE
Brauron
Koropi
Marcopoulo
Glyphada
Thorikos
Laurion
0 5 10 15 km
Cap Sounion

ITINERARY III

THE ENVIRONS OF ATHENS

Kaisariani — Mount Hymettus — Cape Sounion — Laurion — Thorikos — Markopoulo — Brauron — Marathon — Amphiareion.

ONE of the most interesting monuments in the neighbourhood of Athens is the MONASTERY OF KAISARIANI which is only 7 kilometres from the centre and can be reached by taking Vasileos Constandinou Street.

This little monastery is situated in the hollow of a small valley in a delightful setting of pines and cypresses. It was built near a spring whose waters were brought to Athens by conduits in the days of antiquity for they were believed to have healing properties. The conduits have disappeared and all that remains of the fountain is a spout shaped like a ram's head.

The church, consecrated to the Presentation of the Virgin, is on the site of a 5th-century basilica. It was built in the 10th century in alternating rows of brick and stone in the form of a Greek cross with a cupola in the centre resting on four columns. The narthex is surmounted by a shallower cupola and it dates from the 17th century as well as the paracclesion and its campanile. The frescoes of the main body of the church are of the 16th century whilst those of the narthex were executed in 1682 by Yoannis Hypatos.

They belong to the Byzantine tradition and, whilst the *Christ Pantocrator* fills the dome, *The Virgin seated between the Archangels Michael and Gabriel* is in the central apse. The north wall is devoted to a representation of the *Tree of Jesse* and to portraits of the apostles, whilst scenes from The Life of Christ are depicted around the walls beginning with *The Nativity* to the right of the apse.

The court of the monastery is closed on the western side by monastic buildings. These include the kitchen and the refectory which now houses a museum. The structure on this side consists of two storeys with large arcades surmounted by a terrace.

On the south side excavations have brought to light the cells of monks, a bath house with a hypocaust and, on the north side, the entrance to a subterranean room which was probably the ossiary.

Continuing a little further on to the left we come to another small valley where we find the Monastery of Asterion which has been recently restored. The church, in the plan of a Greek cross, was built in the 11th century. In the narthex as well as in the main body of the church are 16th-century frescoes. The apse of the refectory is also decorated with frescoes.

From this point it is possible to drive up to the top of MOUNT HYMETTUS, which is 1,026 metres in altitude. Formerly it was covered with aromatic plants which gave their distinctive flavour to Hymettus honey. Today there is only heather and most of the bees have migrated towards the Pentelikon and the Tourko Vouni.

On the slope of this hill, where there were formerly the famous marble quarries, you may still discover a number of ancient tombs.

Descending towards Athens and following the coast round the Saronic Gulf, the road passes through GLYPHADA with its immense beach which is so popular in the summer. On the shore near the Andonopoulos Restaurant are the ruins of a paleo-Christian Basilica alleged to have been built to com-

9. CAPE SOUNION: TEMPLE OF POSEIDON.

10. BRAURON: PORTICO OF THE SANCTUARY.

memorate the first landing of St. Paul in Greece and erected here by the Apostle.

The route then passes a number of beaches surrounded by umbrella pines and promontories of red rocks before reaching Sounion and the bay of Anavysos from which there is a prospect of CAPE SOUNION and of the columns of the Temple of Poseidon on the summit.

This is one of the most poetic places in Greece for the promontory plunges straight down into the sea, and the remains of the temple dedicated to Poseidon, the god of the sea, and to Athena stand dramatically against the sky.

The sanctuary was originally surrounded by a semicircular wall, the remains of which can still be seen, including those of a fortified gateway which gave access to a little harbour partly hollowed out of the rock for the triremes. There are also ruins of the walls which separated the sanctuary from the Propylaea. These opened out on to a hall with three doors and on to a portico with two columns *in antis*. Built out of tufa in the 6th century B.C., they were restored in marble in the 5th century.

Next to the peribolus the remains of a square room can be distinguished and a large portico with two galleries separated by a line of six interior columns of which five bases still remain in place. Another hall with a portico is set at right angles to the preceding one. On public holidays people used to shelter in the shade of these buildings.

The Temple of Poseidon, which dates from the second half of the 5th century B.C., is on the site of an archaic temple built of tufa whose foundations have been discovered.

Above the double foundations stand fifteen Doric columns which have only sixteen flutings instead of the usual twenty. It was a peripteral temple with six columns on the façade and thirteen at the side and comprised a central *naos* or *cella* with a *pronaos* and an *opisthodome* (recessed rear porch) with two columns *in antis*. A sculptured frieze on the architrave of the *pronaos* depicted the exploits of Theseus, the battles between the Centaurs and the Lapiths and scenes from the lives of the Cyclops of which a few fragments are displayed nearby.

On a low hillock on the south side of the isthmus lie the remains of the temple of Athena Sounias. It was built in the 6th century B.C., and was bordered by an incomplete peristyle. All that remains of it is a plinth of polygonal stones.

Returning to the main road we continue on to LAURION, a small industrial town which thrives on the lead and silver mines which were neglected for centuries. It was thanks to the discovery of these deposits in 484 B.C. that Themistocles was able to build the fleet of 200 triremes which overcame the Persians at Salamis.

The road passes through a pleasant countryside of vines and olive trees whose silver and green foliage contrasts with the red earth and then continues through THORIKOS, a hamlet built on the site of a very ancient Attic city, important because its harbour sheltered the ships which brought timber for the foundries of Laurion. The upper town was surrounded by a rampart of which there remains a fragment flanked by a square tower. Inside the city a theatre has been excavated, a theatre which could accommodate five thousand spectators, and there are also the ruins of a temple of Dionysos, a temple of the two goddesses, Demeter and Kore, two tombs with cupolas and a Mycenaean wall.

A kilometre to the west of this place traces of a fortress erected by the Athenians towards 412 B.C. have been discovered.

After crossing the Plaka Pass, a road to the left leads to the village of Kalyvia, where the churches Taxiarchis, Soteira and Evangheliemos are adorned with frescoes of the school of Giorgios Marcos.

Further on at MARKOPOULO stand the little basilicas of

Haghios Constantinos, Haghia Triada and the church of the Panaghia. Haghia Kyriaki and Haghia Paraskevi stand near the main square. The frescoes may have been painted by Georgios Markos d'Argos.

Two kilometres after leaving Markopoulo by the Porto Raffti road a secondary highway leads to the sanctuary of BRAURON six kilometres away and set in a charming landscape of vines, cypresses and olives.

This sanctuary was consecrated to appease the wrath of Artemis after the slaughtering of a bear, who had killed a young girl in a village of Attica. The goddess had caused a plague and delivered a message by an oracle that she required the inhabitants to consecrate their maidens to her. The festival of Brauronia took place every five years in the springtime. This sanctuary of Artemis was the most ancient in Attica and, according to tradition recorded by Euripides in his *Sacrifice of Iphigenia*, the daughter of Agamemnon was put to death at Brauron.

In the excavation on this site there is, on the left-hand side, a very ancient bridge over the Erasinos and a portico with a stylobate of marble of the second half of the fifth century B.C. whose columns have been set up again. The two wings of this portico enclosed a court bounded to the south by the altar, the *hieron* of Iphigenia and the sacred house.

The rooms which opened out to the south beneath the north gallery were given up to the "she bears" or *arktoi*, the maidens who took part in the festivities in honour of the goddess. The sanctuary seems to have been flooded towards the end of the 4th century B.C. and little by little buried beneath the sands of Erasinos, a circumstance which kept it more or less intact. Excavations have unearthed a propylaeum to the north of this portico. It was part of another building and so it has been possible to restore the entry to the sanctuary there.

On approaching the hill it is now possible to discern the plan of a temple from its foundations. It was a prostyle temple, of the Doric order, comprising a *pronaos*, a *cella* with three naves and an *adyton*.

On the hill itself the small 15th-century *Chapel of Haghios Georgios* contains, in the narthex, fragments of paintings representing St. Timotheon and St. Spiridon.

Ten metres from the temple there is a cutting in the rock forming a kind of passage where one comes upon a little sanctuary composed of two cells which was built of tufa after the grotto behind it had fallen in. A little further on there is a sanctuary more than fifteen metres long comprising four compartments which was ruined when the grotto fell in. The tomb of Iphigenia is reputed to be on this spot. The last structure at the exit of the passage formed by the collapse of the grotto appears to have been the house of the priestesses dedicated to the service of the sanctuary.

On request, the keeper of this site takes visitors round the ruins of a paleo-Christian church with a narthex and exonarthex. It is situated in the middle of a vineyard by the roadside just before coming to Brauron. The round structure on the south side is either the baptistry or a martyrium.

On returning to Markopoulo our route continues towards Koropi and through the Mesogea, the most fertile plain in Attica, where a number of ancient necropolis still subsist.

At Koropi, in the recently restored Church of the Metamorphosis, some Byzantine frescoes of the 10th century have been discovered. This village contains several other little churches decorated with frescoes by Georgios Marcos.

Following the road towards Stavros which gives access to a number of little beaches lost in the pines and lentiscus, we come upon the site of MARATHON where a tumulus was erected to receive the ashes of the 192 Athenians who had died in battle and whose bodies had been burnt together. This monument rises up in the midst of the fields and almond orchards not far from the reedy marshes which line the crescent-shaped bay.

The Persian fleet commanded by Datis and Artaphernes had first of all taken Eretria in Euboea and had then landed in the bay of Marathon, the army which was to march on Athens. Herodotus speaks of 200,000 infantry and 20,000 cavalry. There were in fact only 6,000 foot soldiers and 600 horsemen. The Athenians numbered 9,000 men who were joined by 1,000 Plataeans. After hesitating for a week, Datis decided to attack. The Persians broke through the Greek centre, but in the wings the Athenians and the Plataeans drove back their enemies and were able to attack their main body in reverse forcing them to retreat towards their vessels.

On leaving Marathon we come upon RHAMNONTE, one of the most impressive sites in Attica for it is both forlorn and melancholy in its narrow valley dominated by rugged mountains. Rhamnonte, "a place where the blackthorn flourishes", and the home of the orator Antiphon, was one of the largest townships of the northern highlands of Attica and was celebrated for its Acropolis which guarded the access to the Gulf of Euripeis and also for its sanctuary of Nemesis.

The latter was on a terrace reached by a ramp. On this terrace were two adjacent temples. The little temple or Temple of Themis of the 6th century B.C. is a Doric temple *in antis* with a *pronaos* with two columns.

It was probably built between the years 436 and 432 B.C. by the architect who was responsible for the temple of Sounion and those of Hephaestos and Ares in Athens, but it was not completed. The plinth of a votive statue is the work of Phideas, according to Pausanias, but of his pupil Agora Critos, according to other authorities.

The path, lined with ruined tombs, comes to an end at the gateway of the fortress which is still imposing with its two flanking towers on the hill which it dominates. It is known today as the Ovreo Kastro (Castle of the Jews). Access to the only gateway is reached by a ramp and the approach is protected by two square towers. The walls are of Hellenic facing in blocks of local white marble and date from the 4th century B.C. The outer wall, an irregular rectangle 260 metres long by 120–130 metres wide, follows more or less the outline of the cliffs and the rocky escarpments which dominate the valley. A segment at the south-east corner still rises to a height of four metres. This rampart was flanked by towers, three on the south side, one at the south-east corner and one at the north-west. On the south-west there remains a tower on a lower level. To the south the system to protect the entrance is clearly discernible with two corner towers as well as two flanking towers. From the north-west tower a projection 25 metres long ends in a tower built to prevent the scaling of the cliff face.

The interior is divided into two terraces: on the first there are remains of different constructions and, notably, of a little temple of Dionysus as well as the caves of a theatre where the assemblies of the demes must have been held.

The original Acropolis was built on the second terrace with an oval outer wall of irregular outline dating from the end of the 6th century or perhaps from the 5th century B.C. but it is completely ruined. In the interior the remains of barracks, and cisterns of this period, can still be seen among the shrubs and undergrowth.

The lower town was on the sea shore at the foot of the hill and at the outlet of the stream.

Returning to Marathon we continue through Grammatiko and on to Kalamos where the road to Amphiareion turns off on the left hand side immediately after the church. Soon there is a prospect of a superb landscape over the sea and the island of Euboea, and we come upon a pine clad valley at the bottom of which rise up the ruins of the sanctuary of Amphiaraos or *AMPHIAREION.*

Amphiaraos, hero and prophet of Argos, was one of the seven chieftains who took part in the siege of Thebes. According to legend he was swallowed up with his chariot near this city where he was revered. He was then worshipped in the region of Oropos and his name hallowed in this ravine near to a spring reputed for its healing qualities.

Most of the ruins date from the 4th century B.C. and in spite of the broken columns and the dilapidated ruins the mystery and poetry of this place give us some idea of what it was like in the days when the hero was revered and consulted as an oracle and a healing god.

The first ruins to be seen are those of the Doric Temple of Amphiaraos. In the middle of the *cella* was the table for votive offerings and at the far end the base of the statue. Beyond, an outer portico provided an access to the priests' quarters. In the middle on the north-west side a door opened on to the little room of the oracles.

Ten metres in front of the temple lie the foundations of a monumental altar where sacrifices were made to the gods and to the heroes, whilst four metres further on, tiers of seats were separated from the altar by a conduit: on the right, seven metres from the altar, is the circular orifice of the sacred spring by which Amphiaraos reappeared on earth when he became a god. Those who had been healed by the advice of the oracle threw a piece of gold or silver into the spring and people drank the water in shells, of which many were found in the vicinity.

At the foot of the hill we can see a long terrace with an alignment of the remains of more than thirty plinths of statues; in front of these stretched a long stone bench.

Beyond this bench there is a long portico dating from the beginning of the 4th century. Most of the columns can still be seen, though they are more or less broken up. It was there that patients slept whilst waiting for the dream which would reveal to them the healing remedy. All along the walls there was a marble bench supported by marble feet.

The theatre lies behind the portico. It was hollowed out of the side of the hill and its acoustics are excellent, even though it could accommodate as many as 3,000 spectators. Some of the tiers still subsist as well as five marble seats decorated with bas-relief and bearing inscriptions.

In front of the walls of the stage there has been a reconstruction of the portico serving as a *proscenium* and few can fail to be moved by the beauty of this rustic setting where the pine trees mingle with the ancient ruins.

In a small museum are displayed some fragments of sculpture, some tombstones, a statue of the celebrated doctor Amphilocleos and some Byzantine reliefs.

We can continue on to Kala Oropos, the fishing village which is the embarkation port for the ferry for Nea Psara (Eretria) on the island of Euboea, and from there the motorway provides a direct route to Athens.

11. AMPHIAREION: PORTICO OF THE THEATRE.

12. MONASTERY OF DAPHNI.

13. CORINTH: RUINS OF ANCIENT CORINTH.

14. CORINTH : THE TEMPLE OF APOLLO,

ITINERARY IV

ATHENS TO DELPHI

The Academy of Plato — Daphni — Eleusis — Thebes — Livadia — Skripou — Orchomenus — Cheronea — Hosios Loukas — Arachova — Delphi

THREE kilometres after leaving Athens by the Leoforos Athinon, there is, on the right-hand side, about 100 metres from the road, the site of the Academy, the celebrated school of philosophy founded by Plato. These remains which are more especially of interest to archaeologists are scattered around the *Church of Haghios Triphon.*

The Academy derived its name from a local hero, Akademos or Hekademos, in honour of whom a sanctuary had been built. The vestiges of a building dating from the ancient Helladic period (2300–2000 B.C.), called the house of Akademos was discovered, and in 1958 those of a building of the Geometric Period similar to the Sacred House of Eleusis. An earthen well of the 4th century next to it has been rebuilt.

Athena possessed a temple and a sacred enclosure in this place and the twelve olive trees grown from a cutting of the sacred tree planted by the goddess on the Acropolis of Athens, produced the oil offered to the victors of the Panathenaic Festival. The walls of the enclosure were erected by Hipparchus (527–514 B.C.). There were altars consecrated to other gods, a temple dedicated to Prometheus and three gymnasia for the *ephebi.*

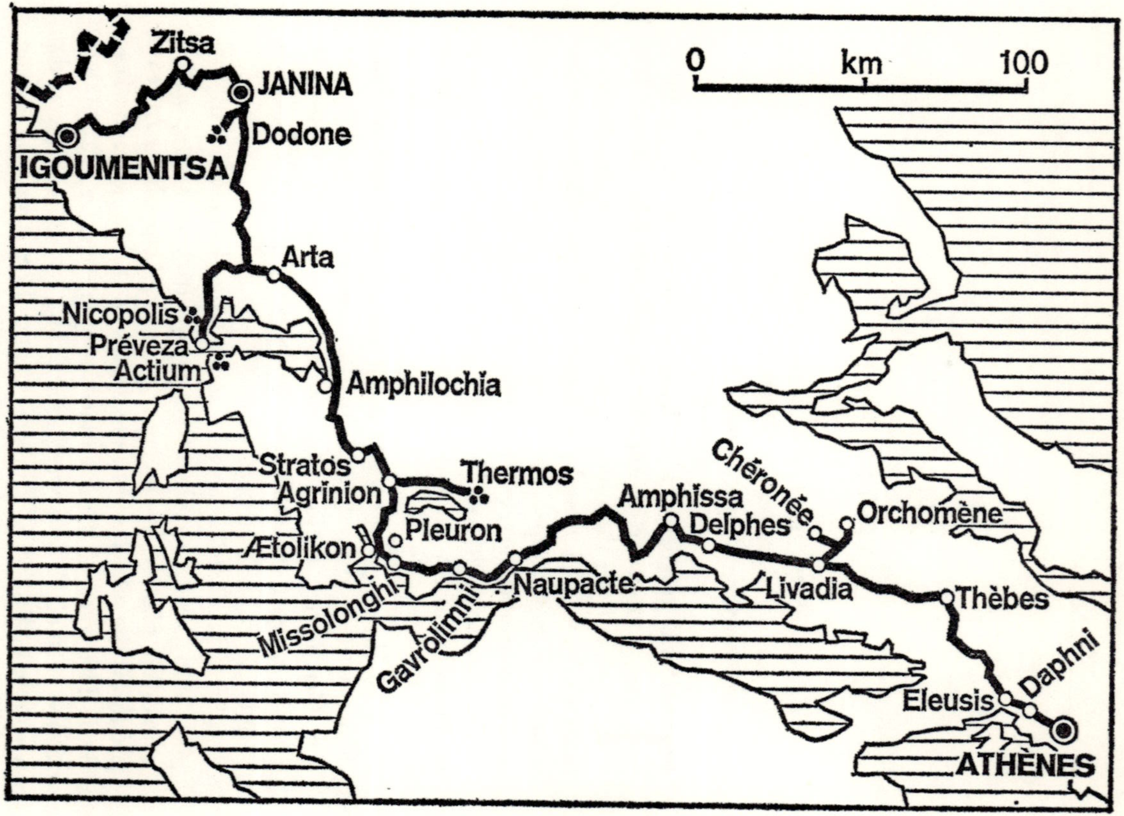
0
km
100
Zitsa
JANINA
Dodone
IGOUMENITSA
Arta
Nicopolis
Préveza
Actium
Amphilochia
Stratos
Agrinion
Thermos
Pleuron
Ætolikon
Missolonghi
Gavrolimni
Naupacte
Amphissa
Delphes
Chéronée
Orchomène
Livadia
Thèbes
Eleusis
Daphni
ATHÈNES

It was towards 388 B.C. that, near the end of his life, Plato founded his school of philosophy. He owned an estate in this district which he had consecrated to the muses and it was there that he taught and was buried. His pupil Xeuxippus and others after him continued the teaching of the master.

Several sections of the road of the Academy to the Dipylon have been excavated. It is lined with tombs, the foundations of the gymnasium restored in the 5th century A.D. and, a little further on, the remains of a square building 40 metres long believed to be the Mouseion or Academy of Plato.

To the east of the academy, on the other side of Lenormant Street, a little chalky hillock covered with trees and oleanders is the Colonus where Sophocles was born. In his *Oedipus at Colonus* he described how the blind Oedipus, led by Antigone, found asylum near the Sanctuary of the Eumenides.

By crossing the Cephisus we come upon the MONASTERY OF DAPHNI, one of the most noteworthy buildings of Byzantine architecture in Greece. It is celebrated for its mosaics of the end of the 11th century A.D.

The monastery, founded in the 5th or 6th century, was consecrated to the Dormition of the Virgin; the name of Daphni is derived from the laurels which grew nearby and evoked the former worship of Apollo whose temple, situated on the same spot, was destroyed about A.D. 395

Rebuilt towards 1080, the monastery was sacked in 1205 by the Crusaders. In 1211 Otto de la Roche installed the Cistercians here. It was here also that the Duke de la Roche and Walter de Brienne were interred. The Cistercians fled from this spot on the arrival of the Turks in 1458, but it was reoccupied in the 16th century by the Orthodox Church to be abandoned once more at the time of the War of Independence.

Some vestiges of the square wall flanked by towers and buttresses subsist. As well as the church, we can see the remains of the monastic buildings, the foundations of a vast refectory with an 11th-century apse, the Great Cistercian cloister backing on to the church and the 16th-century cells surrounding a square courtyard with a cistern.

The 16th-century narthex of the church was partially rebuilt in the 13th century by the Cistercians who were responsible for the arches of the western façade.

It is a church on the plan of a Greek cross following the model of the New Church built in Constantinople by Basil I. In the centre a dome is supported on squinches. The mosaics on the walls and the dome are masterpieces of the 11th and 12th century Byzantine Renaissance which is also exemplified at Hosios Loukas and in the Nea Moni of Chios. At Daphni a humanistic Christian art is notable for its mastery of composition, gracefulness of design, subtlety of form and brilliance of colouring.

The different themes are disposed according to the theological conventions of the period. *Christ Pantocrator*, severe and threatening, appears in all his glory above the prophets in the dome, whilst the squinches are devoted to the *Annunciation*, to *The Nativity of Christ*, to his *Baptism* and to *The Transfiguration*. The Virgin appears in the apse whilst angels, prophets and saints are depicted on the arches, the vaulting and the niches, and other scenes from the Gospels decorate the nave and the narthex. Most impressive of all is the distinguished composition of *The Nativity*, the beauty of the human body in the *Baptism of Christ*, the vigour of *Christ Pantocrator*, the intense emotion expressed in *The Crucifixion* and *The Descent into Hell*, the invention and originality of scenes like *The Assumption of the Virgin*, *The Communion*, *The Last Supper* and *The Day of Judgement*.

The elongated proportions of the figures with their natural gestures and draperies flow with a grace which presupposes a study of the models of antiquity. They are represented with a new realism which is also to be found in the Serbian frescoes of a later date.

The shady park near the monastery is a setting for a tourist pavilion and the vintage festivities which take place in the autumn.

We continue to follow the road to Eleusis. At the 13th kilometre, on the right, a piece of rock, near which there used to be a sanctuary of Aphrodite, is hollowed out for votive niches. A rectangular peribolus formed of a great stone surrounded the temple and several stone constructions of which one was the House of the Pilgrims. We can also make out the remains of a Sacred Way and of an ancient fort.

At the 16th kilometre we can see the first of two sacred lakes dedicated one to Demeter and one to Kore. Only the priests were allowed to fish there or to keep a boat.

We then arrive at ELEUSIS which has become an important industrial town. After the first crossroads we turn to the left for the excavation site.

Eleusis, which was for long the rival of Athens, was a sacerdotal state originated, according to legend, by the king-priest Eumolpos. It was here that Demeter received the hospitality of the king Keleos whilst seeking her daughter Kore, carried off by Hades. In gratitude, the goddess had given to Triptolemus, the king's son, the first grain of corn and she had taught him to cultivate the ground. The Mysteries of Eleusis founded by Eumolpos on the orders of the goddess were inaugurated to perpetuate this gift. The cult of the great goddesses Demeter and Kore made Eleusis famous until the 4th century.

The original large village, which goes back to prehistoric times, was situated upon an eminence and protected by an *enceinte* distinct from the rampart which surrounded the summit of the hill where the Palace of the King and the Acropolis stood.

Conquered by Athens in the course of the 7th century, Eleusis retained certain privileges and the direction of the Mysteries. The principal ministers of the cult of the Great

Goddesses were recruited from the two sacerdotal families, the Eumolpedes and the Keryces. The festivals took place twice a year in February–March and September–October. Aeschylus was born in Eleusis in 515 B.C.

The city which had known a new prosperity under Hadrian and Antoninus Pius was sacked by Alaric in A.D. 395 and the Mysteries were forbidden under Theodosius at the end of the 4th century. The town, which was abandoned after the Byzantine era, was not repopulated until the end of the 18th century.

The ruins of the sanctuary of the Great Goddesses occupy a terrace at the extreme south-east of the Acropolis hill. Access to the sanctuary was forbidden to the uninitiated on pain of death and it was enclosed by a high fortified *enceinte* doubled on the entrance side. Beyond the gates of the city, the Sacred Field where the first seed given by Demeter was sown, encloses the threshing floor and the altar of Triptolemus.

Near the entrance to the excavations, a vast paved esplanade of the 2nd century A.D. is filled with the ruins of buildings and the galleries which surrounded them. To the right lie the remains of the foundations of the two neighbouring altars of the Temple of Artemis Propylaea and of Poseidon Pater belonging to the Doric temple dedicated to these two divinities. The temple was built in the Roman era partly upon the site of an 8th-century sanctuary of the Geometric era. We can still see the rectangular ditch where the victims offered to the Chlonian divinities were burnt. Beyond this spot are the ruins of a portico.

We then arrive at the Great Propylaea built in Pentelic marble under Antoninus Pius (A.D. 138–161) in imitation of those of the Acropolis of Athens. They present, outside, a Doric portico of six columns of which sections lie on the esplanade. Amongst these we can see a great carved medallion with a portrait of Antoninus Pius.

The Great Propylaea stands on the site of a former gateway

out into the outer *enceinte* constructed at the beginning of the 5th century B.C. and restored by the Romans.

To the left of the Propylaea, between the ruins of a rectangular tower and the portico, are the Callichoros wells mentioned in the Homeric hymn to Demeter and also mentioned by Euripides and Pausanias. It was around these wells that the women of Eleusis sang and danced for the first time in honour of Demeter.

We can then see the vestiges of one of the two triumphal arches on either side of the esplanade and the basin of a fountain which may have served for the ablutions of the pilgrims.

On the other side of the Propylaea we shall find the second triumphal arch and a postern which crossed the rampart, dating from the time of Pisistrates. We then end up at an ancient street flanked by the Pompeion where the sacred chariots were kept, and finally reach the great Propylaea and the House of the Heralds.

Next we come to the little Propylaea built on the site of a fortified gateway in the 6th-century *enceinte*. They were built on the orders of the proconsul, Appius Claudius Pulcher, friend of Cicero. This dates from 54 B.C.

We then climb up by the Sacred Way, paved in the Roman era with white marble and Eleusis stone, and leave to the right, in the cliff face, two grottoes preceded by a terrace closed in by a wall. It is the Plutonion, or Sanctuary of Pluto, and it was doubtless at this place that Persephone disappeared into the infernal regions deep in the earth.

The Temple of the God used to stand in front of the larger of the two grottoes.

Further on, steps cut in the rock lead to a platform where there may have stood the altar of the two goddesses with its round ditch for libations.

To the left, can be seen a rather confused conglomeration of ramparts and buildings of various epochs and to the right, a megaron which was perhaps the Temple of Kore—Persephone.

The Sacred Way ends in the entrance to the *Telesterion*, the initiation chamber of the Mysteries.

If the rape of Persephone, and his six months' sojourn in Hades, symbolizes the winter and the mourning period of Nature, the Mysteries were concerned with a moral and religious doctrine which was manifested more especially in the form of a sacred drama and of revelations upon the voyage of the soul into the underworld.

The ruins which we see belong to different structures from primitive to Roman times. They comprise a room a little more than 50 metres long and partly cut into the rock. The ceiling was supported by 6 rows of 7 columns and on each of the sides, 8 rows of tiers, some cut into the rock, others made of stones which were inset. There was room for 3,000 people.

A portico opens on the south-east side. It was begun in 350 B.C. and was called by the name of its architect Philon. The lateral stairways lead to the megaron where the sacred objects were kept and displayed.

From the *Telesterion* we can go to the museum in the courtyard where we shall find several fragments of statues from the sanctuary: a sarcophagus of the Roman period on which is depicted the Boar of Calydon put to death by Meleager and Atalanta, and the head of a horse.

In the interior there is a collection of statues and reliefs of different periods, some of them Archaic, some Roman and a number of ceramics found at Eleusis.

There is no point in climbing up to the Acropolis where the excavations can only be of interest to specialists.

On departing from Eleusis we leave the road to Corinth to the left and find some 20 kilometres further on, at the entry to the Kaza Pass, the fortress of Eleutheres on the right. It rises up on a hillock where it defended the road from Thebes to Athens. The *enceinte* reinforced with towers with two

15. CORINTH : RUINS OF ANCIENT TEMPLE.

16. MONASTERY OF HOSIOS LOUKAS.

17. DELPHI : THEATRE.

18. DELPHI : THOLOS.

storeys date from the 4th century B.C. and is amongst the best preserved ruins in Greece.

Near the fortress and on the site of the former town of Eleutheres, the remains of a temple and of two basilicas with three naves of the 5th or 6th century have been brought to light.

We then go over the pass of Dryos Kephalae from which there is an extensive view over Parnassus, the Boeotian lakes, Eubuea, Koromoli, Helicon and Eliatias, the highest summit of the Citheron hills. It was here the Laios abandoned Oedipus when the oracle of Delphi had revealed that his union with Jocasta would bear a son who would kill him.

A little further on we pass a road to the left which goes to PLATAEA where in 479 B.C. the Greeks defied the troops of Mardonius, the General of Xerxes. Only fragments of the town and its *enceinte* remain.

We then arrive in THEBES, the legendary city clothed in so much romance in our imagination that its reality cannot fail to disappoint us. Since the ancient city was ruined again and again, only a few fragments are visible.

According to tradition, the Phoenician, Cadmos, founded the palace of Cadmos and the whole complex of buildings later took the name of Thebes.

In historic times, Thebes, which tried to bring about the union of the larger villages of Bocotia dominated by an aristocracy of wealthy peasants, was opposed to the democratic spirit of Athens. It imposed its hegemony upon other towns in Greece at the time of Epaminondas and of Pelopidas from 371–362 B.C., but after the death of Epaminondas its fortune changed to tragedy for the city was systematically destroyed in 336 B.C. by Alexander of Macedon. The town rose up again, but thenceforth it only played a secondary role, as can be seen by the huge Frankish tower of the second half of the 13th century, built by Nicholas II of St. Omer. It was part of a fortress which the Catalans destroyed in 1311.

Vestiges of the Gate of Electra, of the Palace of Cadmos and of the Ismenion can be seen beyond the Museum.

We continue towards LIVADIA situated at the foot of two hills of which one is crowned with a Frankish castle. Handwoven blankets in brilliant colours hang to dry over the little Turkish bridges which cross the streams flowing through the town. In the days of antiquity it was renowned for the infernal gorge of Hercyna and the oracle of Trophonios. We can see also two springs, the Mnemosyne, the spring of memory, and the Lethe, the spring of forgetfulness.

The gorge itself is rather charming with its plane trees and little cafés along the edge of the torrent. We can also visit the springs and the cave of the Trophonios described by Pausanias, as well as the fortress built in 1311 by the Catalans. It comprises three *enceintes*, the first defended by a great exterior bastion which is doubtless a later addition, and ends up to the south in a great square tower which protected a postern now walled up. To the east it terminates in an enormous tower which rises up at the entrance to the gorge in whose walls we can still see many antique fragments. This tower was linked to the *enceinte* by two curtain walls.

The second *enceinte*, buttressed by three towers, was, like the first, defended by a barbican protecting the gateway. In the court beyond the modern chapel, rise up the high walls of the fortress keep.

ORCHOMENUS is only 13 kilometres away from Livadia. It was one of the richest and most ancient of the towns of Greece in the Heroic Age. It was the capital of Minyae and the home of a brilliant civilization. Destroyed by the Thebans in 364 B.C. and in 349 B.C., it was rebuilt by Philip of Macedon and Alexander.

We shall first visit, at the end of the village of SKRIPOU, the Monastery of the Dormition of the Virgin whose church was built in 874 on the site of the Temple of Graces which is venerated at Orchomenus.

The Church of the Theotokos is a basilica with three aisles with barrel vaulting separated by walls pierced with doors at the ends. The vaulting which buttresses them transversally to the north and to the south, overlaps the alignment of the exterior walls; the central nave is higher than the side ones and a dome is raised above the crossing of the transept.

A hundred metres to the south-west of the monastery stands the Treasury of Minyas named after the legendary ancestor of the Minyans.

It is a Mycenaean tomb with a dome and an entrance passage with a pyramidal door with a lintel of blue schist and a rotunda or *tholos*. In the middle lie the remains of a marble pedestal and, to the east, the entrance to the funeral chamber with a rectangular cell cut out of the rock.

We next come to the *enceinte* of the Hellenic town which dates from the 7th century B.C.; the Minyan town is on a lower level. We shall find in the area of the Christian cemetery the substructure of a temple of the Geometric Age and, on a second terrace, the remains of a Temple to Asclepios and the terraces of the Macedonian town rebuilt by Philip. Here the polygonal masonry is two metres thick. The Acropolis, reduced to a square keep, is of more carefully dressed stone.

We can now go to CHERONEA where Philip of Macedon defeated a coalition of Greek cities in 338 B.C., a victory which enabled him to conquer all Greece. In the village we can see the marble lion which surmounted the tombs where Thebans collected the bones of the dead of the Sacred Battalion, a Little Museum and vestiges of the city of Cheronea where Plutarch lived and died (A.D. 46–120).

We now take the road to Delphi but after 24 kilometres we turn to the left to drive 13 kilometres to the MONASTERY OF HOSIOS LOUKAS, one of the most remarkable groups of Byzantine buildings in the whole of Greece.

This monastery was not consecrated to the Evangelist St. Luke, as was thought for so long, but to a local saint, Loukas the stiriote, or Hosios Loukas who died in 946 or 949. The church which he had erected in 942 became a place of pilgrimage and his disciples built upon his tomb in 951 a church dedicated to St. Barbara, a funeral chapel and a monastery.

In the 11th century these constructions were replaced by those which we see today and which comprise two churches side by side, a large one dedicated to *Hosios Loukas* and a smaller one dedicated to *the Virgin Theotokos, Virgin Mother of God.*

The large church is composed of a narthex, of a nave flanked with collaterals surmounted by a *gynaeceum* where the women sat during services, of a transept with a central dome and a tripartite choir flanked by two supplementary chapels.

The dome is linked to the square base by dummy corners. It was the first of its type to be built in Greece and this is why its foundation is attributed to an emperor, if not to Romanus II, at least to Basilius II who would have honoured a vow made by his father. It is on a plan characteristic of the architecture of Constantinople: a square with an inscribed Greek cross but with narrower arms and more perigonal supports. The groined vaults, niches hollowed out of the lateral faces of the sanctuary and the narthex, the galleries and the great windows all denote an architect from Constantinople, but the ashlar walls and the brick decoration is typically Greek.

The walls, the vaults and the domes were entirely covered with mosaics; those which disappeared after an earthquake which damaged the structure in 1659 were replaced by frescoes in the 17th century.

These mosaics are perfect examples of the hieratic style of the end of the 10th century or the beginning of the 11th. The presence among the mosaics of a portrait of Nicon the Penitent allows us to date them precisely. They were obviously the work of artists from Constantinople or Salonica. In the central dome, the Pantocrator was originally surrounded with prophets, but this part has been replaced by frescoes. *Pentecost* occupies the vault above the altar, whereas the conch of the apse is decorated with *the Theotokos with the Child upon her knee*. In the interior of the *naos*, four evangelist scenes have been depicted: *The Annunciation*, which has disappeared, *The Nativity, The Presentation in the Temple*, and *The Baptism*. In the narthex we can see *The Crucifixion*, *The Descent into Hell*, *The Washing of the Feet*, and *The Doubting of St. Thomas*.

In these compositions the dramatic force is stressed by the extreme restraint of the treatment. In *The Crucifixion*, for example, the number of people and objects depicted are reduced to a minimum: Christ, his Mother, St. John, Golgotha below the cross with the skull of Adam, the sun and the moon, but it has such spiritual significance that the actual Passion seems to be enacted before our eyes. The sadness of Mary and John with their stiff and formal stocky bodies is no less moving for being contained within them. The colour, without any contrasting light, is sober with touches of monochrome, of brownish grey and white for the body of Christ, of greenish yellow for the faces of John and the Virgin. This formalized beauty gives full rein to spiritual expression.

We must also notice the pavement in polychrome marble, the marble iconostasis and four ikons dating from 1570 painted by the Cretan artist, Damaskinos.

In the crypt, which was the original Church of St. Barbara, are a few frescoes in a bad state of deterioration, and five tombs, among which the tomb of Hosios Loukas was recently restored.

Nearby the *Church of the Theotokos* is decorated with frescoes, some of which date from the original construction of the church.

Finally, as well as admiring the refectory which has recently been restored, we can appreciate the whole admirable effect of the two churches with their double and triple bays heightened by slender columns and the dressing of brick and stone.

We then come to ARACHOVA, a picturesque village on

the side of the mountain above the valley of the Pleistos. It is through the pass of Arachova that the road which linked Boeotia to the Sanctuaries of Delphi ran, and authors of antiquity tell how the Persians and the Gauls who had ventured along this route in A.D. 480 and in 279 B.C. were miraculously arrested at the very gates of Delphi.

Soon we see the first ruins of DELPHI appear and then the site in all its sublime nobility. It is at Delphi rather than anywhere else that we can evoke the mystery of the sacred rites of ancient Greece in this splendid setting of tragic solitude which contrasts so greatly with the sensual softness of the green mass of olive trees which cover the Sacred Plain.

Delphi was a seat of worship from the very remotest antiquity and it is claimed that from the 15th century B.C. the goddesses were venerated here. The goddess Ge, the Earth and the Underworld, of whom we find little images in terracotta, expressed herself by the sound of trees and waters, sounds whose interpretation produced the oracles and the oracles were guarded by the serpent Python.

Apollo before the end of the Mycenaean epoch, about the 12th century B.C., killed the python and appropriated the oracle. But it was during the 8th and 7th centuries that Delphi became the great panhellenic centre. No war, nor expedition was undertaken without first consulting the oracle who gave wise and precise information and advice.

During the first Sacred War of 590 B.C., a coalition of Greek states freed the oracle from the guardianship of Krissa, a little town in the plain to which the territory of Delphi belonged. From then on an interhellenic council administered the sanctuary and the Pythian festival was celebrated every four years. The Delphic oracle enjoyed a period of unbelievable prosperity with the construction of the first "treasuries" which housed the offerings.

The temple was destroyed in 548 B.C. by a fire and partly reconstructed in 539. In 514 the Alcemonides undertook its completion. In the museum we can see several fragments of the sculpture of this temple which kept the same aspect until the end of paganism, that is to say until the 6th century of our era.

Apollo had disdained the uncertain whisperings of the laurel leaves, the murmuring of wandering bees and the images reflected in the waters of the springs, to return to the sacred deliriums of the Pythia.

The consultants drew lots for the order in which they would be interviewed, after having paid a special tax which differed according to their nationality or whether they came to consult on their own account or on behalf of their city. The Pythia first purified herself at the Castalian Fountain, and then when she had burnt in the temple the laurel and grain of barley, she descended into the depths of the Divine Dwelling to a low chamber called the Adyton. There close to the *omphalos* and seated upon a Tripod, she drank water taken from the Cassotis Fountain and chewed laurel leaves. She was overcome by a prophetic delirium and she entered into a trance under the influence of an inspiring exhalation. From the room which was reserved for them, the consultants were able to see the fumes whose fragrance was "comparable to the sweetest of perfumes". They could make out a few of the words uttered by the Pythia but it was the priests who interpreted the answers and each consultant was given a small text which was a kind of short, ambiguous and obscure poem whose sense was explained by the Exegetists.

The Pythia was chosen from the old and poor women of Delphi who were of good stock. She was obliged to lead an austere monastic life during her time of office.

During the Wars of the Medes and Persians, even though the Oracle had not actually encouraged the resistance of the Greeks, the prestige of Delphi remained intact. Thanks to its ambiguity it was equally successful in keeping Delphi out of the wars between Sparta and Athens. But in the 4th century the most awful catastrophies befell Delphi. In 373 B.C. an earthquake shattered the temple, but subscriptions flowed in from the whole Greek world to restore it. This restoration was interrupted by the third Sacred War between 356 and 346. Accused by the Thebans, the Phocians were condemned to pay an exorbitant fine for having ploughed up some sections of the Sacred Plain. The resistance of the Phocians continued for ten years. Their Strategus (or General) Phillomelus pillaged the Sacred Treasury and built a fortress at Delphi, but finally the Macedonians replaced the Phocians in the Amphictyonic Council and sentenced them to a fine which was used to reconstruct the temple. Between 339 and 338, the time of the new Sacred War, the fourth, Philip of Macedon undertook to punish the people of Amphissa for having cultivated the Sacred Plain. Philip invaded Greece and took the opportunity to subdue the whole country after his victory at Cheronea in 338 over the Thebans and the Athenians.

The Macedonians were succeeded by the Aetolians who, in 279 B.C., saved Greece from the Gaulish invasion. They became the most powerful people of Greece and Delphi acquired a new splendour, becoming the religious and intellectual capital of the whole of Greece.

In 191 B.C., the Romans expelled the Aetolians and guaranteed autonomy to Delphi which continued to receive tributes and statues. But decadence had already set in. In 91 B.C. the temple was burnt down by the Medes. In 86, Sulla demanded back the Sacred Treasure under pretext of financing the war against Mithridates. If Domitian repaired the temple, Nero carried off 500 statues. Thanks to the generosity of Hadrian, Herodes Atticus and the Antonines, the ancient Delphic Sanctuary was reinstated and assumed a new brilliance in the 2nd century of our era. But the Christian emperors, Constantine and Theodosius II, appropriated the treasures to decorate their new capital of Constantinople and the banishment of paganism in 371 by Theodosius completed the fall of Delphi.

19. MYCENAE: LION GATE.

20. MYCENAE: TOMB OF AGAMEMNON.

21. NEMEA.

22. TIRYNS.

On leaving the village we come to a museum where, in place of the masterpieces described by Pausanias, and of which nothing remains today, is a collection of works which are no less admirable: the frieze of the treasury of Sithanos; the Auriga of Polyzalos still in an archaic pose but noble and serene; the *metopes* from the treasury of Sicyon, and also from the Treasury of the Athenians; sculpture from the Temple of Apollo.

By following the road to Arachova we soon arrive at the sanctuary of the Pythian Apollo which, as usual, was surrounded by a wall with several doorways.

The main gate, approached by 5 steps, gave access to the Sacred Way. This latter, 4 or 5 metres wide, wound in the direction of the Sanctuary with steeply inclined rises which were very slippery in spite of the ridges which replace the Hellenic Steps. On each side rose up votive monuments or treasuries built by the Greek cities to house the offerings of the citizens or of groups. These edifices were a witness to the piety, but also to the prosperity and power of the towns which had them built, as well as of the bitter rivalry which divided them. After their victory over Athens, the Spartans set up an *ex-voto*, to the glory of their admirals and generals, right in front of the monument commemorating the Triumph of the Athenians over the Persians at Marathon. Thirty-five years later, the Arcadians, victors in their turn over the Spartans, erected in front of the arrogant monument to Lysander, a row of statues of their national heroes.

We should notice, to the right, beyond the entrance gate, the remains of the base of the Bull of Corcyra, a bronze work executed about 480 B.C. by Theopropos of Aegina, which Corcyra consecrated with the proceeds from an enormous catch of tunny fish. Then we come to the *ex-voto* of the Arcadians, composed of a row of bronze statues of Apollo and the mythical heroes and heroines of Arcadia. Then a statue of an Arcadian general. The Spartan Generals and Admirals came behind the *ex-voto* of the Arcadians; the foundations of a great niche can still be seen which held the 37 statues of the *ex-voto* of the Lacedemonians. Behind the Dioscures stood statues of Zeus, Apollo, Artemis, Poseidon crowning Lysander, the conqueror of Aegos-Potami, the Divine Agias, the pilot Hermon.

Opposite these monuments, to the left of the Sacred Way, were the *ex-voto* of the Athenians which comprised 16 statues, of which the oldest were attributed to Phidias, then the *ex-voto* of Argos, dedicated to the seven leaders of the expedition against Thebes and the Dorian horse which recalls the Trojan Horse.

We then see along the Sacred Way two semicircular foundations, supporting two monuments of Argos, one of the kings to the right and one of the Epigones to the left. The *exedra* of the kings, which was 12 metres in its interior diameter, contained 20 statues of the ancient kings and queens of Argos. It had been erected a little after 369 B.C., on the occasion of the foundation of Messena, to outshine the monument of the Navarchae. That of their successors, the seven Epigoni, was erected in about 460 B.C.

The niches which we see beyond the *ex-voto* of the kings of Argos have not been definitely identified, but on the other side we shall find the *ex-voto* of the Tarentians. It was composed of bronze statues representing the horses and the Messapian captives, the work of Ageladas of Argos. There remain four plinths of statues commemorating a victory over the Messapians. Then came the Treasury of Sicyon, built at the end of the 6th century, whose plan can still be distinguished, and of which there still remain four well-preserved metopes, and the Treasury of Siphnos, constructed in about 525 B.C. thanks to the prosperity of the gold mines of this little island. It was decorated with a sculptured frieze which can be seen in the Museum.

Here, where the Sacred Way takes a first bend, are several

monuments: the Treasury of the Boeotians and that of the Thebans. These were built before the Treasury of the Athenians which has been re-erected and should give us an idea of what the different aedicules, standing side by side, might have looked like. Consecrated between 490 and 485 B.C., it was built with the tithe of the booty taken from the Persians at Marathon. It is a Doric structure in Paros marble which was decorated with sculpture (now in the Museum) depicting the exploits of Hercules, and of Theseus and scenes from the War of the Greeks against the Amazons.

Opposite we find the Treasury of Syracuse erected at the end of the 5th century B.C., after the defeat of the expedition of Nicias and Alcibiades.

Beyond the Treasury of the Athenians, we come to the Treasury of the Cnidians, the *Bouleuterion* or Senate of Delphi where the 15 senators and 8 *trytanes* sat. Higher up, at the foot of a supporting wall, we find the Sanctuary of the Earth, where the seat of the primitive Oracle of Ge and of her daughter Thea is guarded by the serpent Python.

A circle of great slabs of rocks, surrounded by a little irregular peribolus, bounds the Themenos of the Earth which includes a spring. A projecting rock, formed by a fissure, was the rock of the Sybil who was believed to have prophesied most successfully before the time of Apollo. Close to the rock of the Sybil is the rock where Leto had cried to her son, Apollo, to kill Python so that they could carry off the oracle.

On another rock at the foot of the supporting wall, rose up the column of the Naxians, 10 metres high with 44 flutings and surmounted by a sphinx. It was consecrated in about 550 B.C.

The Sacred Way then crossed a circular area 16 metres in diameter, formerly surrounded by benches and seats, where the sacred drama of the murder of the serpent Python by Apollo was enacted during the Pythian festival.

A path which lies to the south-west leads to the Treasury of

Cyranus, situated close to the peribolus, while to the north-west, against the supporting wall of the terrace of the temple, is to be found the porch of the Athenians, erected after 478 to house the trophies which were doubtless taken from the Persians. It stood on a substructure with three steps which supported eight graceful Ionic columns in Paros marble of which three still stand.

We should note the beautifully dressed masonry of the supporting wall on which the Ancients engraved more than 800 official acts concerning, for the most part, the liberation of slaves between 200 B.C. and A.D. 100. It had been erected after the destruction of the ancient temple in 548 when they had decided to rebuild it on a larger scale. The terrace was enlarged and this was why the wall, constructed in the second half of the 6th century, was partly on the ancient *temenos* of the Earth, of which the upper part disappeared.

Towards 475 B.C. it was surmounted by 20 Archaic Apollos offered by the Cnidian colonists of the Lipari (Aeolian) islands to commemorate a naval victory over the Etruscans.

The Sacred Way then passed in front of the Treasury of the Corinthians which Herodotus attributed to the tyrant Cypselos (657–627 B.C.) and which was the most ancient building of its kind. It contained a bronze palm which stood above a floor covered with serpents and frogs.

After a second bend, the Sacred Way, paved here with huge slabs, goes straight up towards the temple, bordered to the right by the ruins of votive monuments among which is the *ex-voto* of Platea, consecrated by the Greeks with the tithes of the booty taken from the Persians after the Battle of Platea in 475 B.C. This tripod of gold, placed on a column of bronze, rose above a circular plinth. The column had the shape of a piece of rope formed by the entwining of three serpents whose heads supported the Tripod, itself surmounted by a great golden vase. The Tripod was carried off by the Phocians and the Emperor Constantine had the column taken to Constantinople where we can still see it, damaged, and known under the name of the Serpentine Column, in the entrance to the Hippodrome.

Near the Tripod of Platea was the *ex-voto* of the Rhodians with a Chariot of the Sun, then statues of two kings of Pergamum, Eumenes II and Attala I.

The Sacred Way then reaches a crossroads called the Tripod, once surrounded by several rows of offerings which have disappeared. The most remarkable were the statues of two tyrants of Syracuse, Gelo and Hieron and of their brothers, whilst the column of Acanthus or of the Thyades, a kind of funeral cloumn, is in a good state of preservation, though incomplete. It was composed of four monuments bearing tripods and victories in gold which weighed no less than 50 talents (about 1,855 kilograms).

Then we see the Treasury of Acanthus to the right and, on a little esplanade which stretches in front of the temple, the great square base of Apollo Sitalcas: the plinth of the *ex-voto* of Aristaineta and the base of the bronze palm of Eurymedon. This palm, surmounted by a statue of Athena, was consecrated to the Athenians after their victory over the Persians near the mouth of the Eurymedon in 468 B.C. The pillar of Prusias, King of Bithynia, which stands against the base of the palm, has been restored. It was surmounted by the statue of a king.

We then come to the ruins of the Temple of Apollo in front of which are the remains of the great altar to Apollo constructed by the Greeks of Chios. It had three steps of black marble and was faced with slabs of white marble. Right against the altar, they set up, in the 2nd century B.C., the tall pillar which bore a golden statue of the King of Pergamum, Eumenes II, given by the Aeolians.

The temple of the 4th century was a peripteral Doric temple with six columns in tufa, stuccoed on the façade, and fifteen on the sides with two columns between the *antas* the *pronaos* and of the *opisthodome*. The temple contains besides, an adyton, a subterranean cell which contained the omphalos and the prophetic properties, the *oikos*, waiting-room for the consultants, and the *opisthodome* which communicated with the *pronaos*. The podium and the peristyle are intact and several columns have been re-erected. In primitive times the god only gave audience once a year, on the seventh of Bysios, the eighth month of the Delphic year (February–March).

We will now direct our steps towards the theatre, climbing up the stairway at the extremity of the Sacred Way. Near here was discovered the bronze Auriga of the *ex-voto* of Polyzalos, which had been swallowed up by debris during the earthquake of 373. More to the west, lie the remains of a little sanctuary to Poseidon and also of the buildings constructed in the Temenos of Dionysos, the ruins of an *exedra* and of the monument of the Thessalians, built thanks to the generosity of Dachos II. It was executed in order to consecrate to Apollo nine statues illustrating the genealogy of his family. One is in a good state, that of Agias, his great-grandfather, often a victor at the Pancracea. This is in marble and a replica of the bronze original which was doubtless the work of Lysippus.

We now leave the theatre for the stadium which was built in the 5th century B.C. and, remodelled in the Roman era, it could hold 7,000 spectators. It was hollowed into a slope which retains the tiers to the north while those to the south are established on an artificial embankment which has been carried away by the falling rubble. A Roman triumphal arch formed a background to the stadium and four of the pillars which supported the three arches still remain. The northern slope had 12 tiers separated from the gateway by a *podium* which surmounted a gate and by a passage with a stone border running right round the stadium. Thirteen stairways led to the upper corridor. The upper seats had backs. Herodes Atticus defrayed the expense of putting in stone seats. The original ones were of earth like those at Olympia. A rostrum, with seats with backs, marks the site of the *proedria* where the president and judges of the games sat.

If we continue to follow the road to Arachova we shall arrive at the Castalian Spring just where the road takes a sharp turn. Its façade can be seen cut in the rock a few metres to the left at the mouth of a cleft in the Phraedriades. Certain legends give this as the lair of the Python. It must have been consecrated to the cult since the base of a statue to the goddess Ge has been found here.

The Greeks boasted of the purity of the water from the spring whose façade is decorated with seven marble pilasters supporting an entablature. The water wells up from the foot of the façade in a multitude of little rills; they collect in a narrow tank from which they flow out from seven spouts (which were doubtless decorated with masks of lions) before falling into a basin hollowed out of the rock.

Five hundred metres from the spring, a little path goes down between the olive trees towards a terrace and the ruins of a gymnasium constructed in the 4th century B.C. to replace an Archaic building. It was repaired by the Romans. Athletes trained here before participating in the Stadium Games.

On the upper terrace, a long covered gallery bordered an open-air running track, which enabled the athletes to train, sheltered from the sun and the rain.

The competitors were oiled and massaged in the *palestra* on the lower terrace. There were also rest rooms and a round pool for cold baths. Hot baths were an addition of the Roman era.

A pathway running below the road enables one to visit the Sanctuary of Athena whom the Delphians worshipped as Keeper of the Temple. We first come to a building of the 5th century B.C. which was the dwelling of the priests, then the new Temple of Athena Pronaia, built in the 4th century to replace the former ruined temple. It was a peripteral Doric temple without an *opisthodome*, whose interior columns of the *pronaos* were in the Ionic style. It consisted of two chambers opening on to a corridor.

We then reach the most interesting monument of the Marmaria, the celebrated *Tholos* or marble rotunda, one of the most beautiful of the monuments of Delphi and a work in the Attic style of the first quarter of the 4th century B.C. This graceful edifice, whose purpose is uncertain, was surrounded by a Doric peristyle of 20 columns of which three have been re-erected; it surrounded a *cella* which was circular in plan. The wall of the interior was decorated with Corinthian half columns and the floor was paved with black marble. The two carved metopes of the entablature, very much damaged, have been replaced by casts, and the cornice has been completed by two casts of the preserved fragments.

We then see the ruins of the Treasury of Marseilles, an edifice in the Ionic style built between 535 and 530 B.C. whose decoration recalls that of the Treasury of Siphnos. The broken-down columns had capitals decorated with palms. Nearby was another treasury in the Doric style, erected in marble on foundations of limestone between 490 and 460 B.C. A quadrangular altar stands in front of the two treasuries.

Our visit to the Marmaria ends at the ancient Temple of Athena Pronaia in front of which ran the Sacred Way which led to the sanctuary of Apollo. It was built at the beginning of the 5th century B.C. on the site of a more ancient temple. We can distinguish several biscuit-shaped capitals of the Archaic temple destroyed in 480 by a fall of rock. In 1905, after a terrible storm, the same thing occurred, and three huge rocks crushed 12 columns and the east side of the peristyle of the 5th-century temple which was a Doric peripteral hexastyle temple in tufa.

23. ARGOS : THEATRE.

24. EPIDAURUS : THEATRE.

ITINERARY V

THE PELOPONNESUS I—MEGARA TO SPARTA

Megara — Corinth — Nemea — Mycenae — Argos — Midea — Tiryns — Nauplia — Epidaurus — Lerna — Tripolis — Tegea — Sparta.

SETTING off from Athens by the road that leads to Daphni and Eleusis which has already been described in Itinerary IV, we must branch off to the left towards Corinth after passing through Eleusis.

Shortly before reaching the 41st kilometre, there is a prospect of MEGARA which was one of the most celebrated cities of ancient Greece. Her sailors founded many wealthy colonies, including more especially Selinunte, Megara Hublaia in Sicily, and Byzantium and Chalcidon to the east. Ravaged in the wars between Athens and the cities of the Peloponnese, Megara began to decline, and today it is little more than a small country town spread out over the two hills which are the site of the ancient city.

Megara became independent in the 8th century, and it was then that her colonies were developed. From 640 to 600 B.C., she was under the dominion of Theagenes, a popular leader who became a tyrant. He embellished the city and constructed the aqueduct, the remains of which can still be seen. Towards 570 there were conflicts with Athens, but eventually the presence of an Athenian garrison was accepted in order to ward off threatened attacks from Corinth, and it was during this period that the Long Walls that linked up the city to its port of Nicaea were constructed. Ten years later the people of

Patras
Ægion
Xylocastron
Mégaspilaïon
Eleusis
Mégare
Kyllini
Sycione
ATHÈNES
Corinthe
Gastouni
PÉLOPONNÈSE
Némée
Loutra Kyllini
Mycènes
Médéa
Pyrgos
Olympie
Argos
Tirynthe
Lerne
Epidaure
Karytaina
Tripolis
Nauplie
Andritsaina
Tégée
Bassæ
Mégalopolis
Méligala
Filiatra
Sparte
Kalamata
Messène
Géraki
Pylos
Platsa
Méthoni
Koroni
Gythion
Monemvasie
Aéropolis
Yérolimin
Cap Matapan
0 km 50

Megara drove away the Athenians with the help of allies in the Peloponnesus. In 432, Pericles was responsible for a decree which excluded the Megarans from trading in the markets of Attica, and this was one of the causes of the Peloponnesian War. Whilst Athenian ships blockaded the harbour, their troops ravaged the territory of Megara. In 427, Nicias built the causeway that linked up the Island of Minos to the mainland. In the course of the 5th century A.D., Diogenes, a General of the Emperor Anastasius, repaired the fortifications of Megara, but from that time the fortunes of the city began to decline.

The principal square is doubtless on the site of the ancient *agora*, but the only remains of any interest are those of the aqueduct and of the Fountain of Theagenes near the church.

Continuing on our way, we pass by the Skironian Rocks, high cliffs from which the brigand Skiron used to throw travellers into the sea. Theseus killed him in precisely the same way.

Further on, the village of Haghi Theodori is on the site of the Port, Krommyon, which was a satellite of Corinth. According to legend it was here that Theseus killed the Sow Krommyon which fed on human flesh.

After crossing the Corinth Canal which was built in 1882 on the lines of the plan drawn up by the Emperor Nero, we arrive at the modern city which was entirely rebuilt after the earthquake of 1928, and is of no interest whatsoever. The ruins of ancient Corinth can be reached by taking a road to the left which passes in front of the ancient port of Lechaion. Here have been cleared the ruins of a 5th-century basilica which was the largest church of the Greek world. It was preceded by a huge courtyard surrounded on three sides by a continuous covered passage, and on the fourth by an atrium with a semi-circular *peridromos*. Its portico was preceded by a narthex flanked to the north by two structures which appear to have been mausoleums. The church had three aisles separated by two lines of columns.

After crossing through some of the vineyards which produce the celebrated grapes of Corinth, dried and sold as currants, we come upon the village of Paleo-Corinthos where a road on the right leads to the principal field of excavations.

Ancient *CORINTH* extended over a small plateau which overlooked the narrow plain at the foot of the Acrocorinth, the hill which served as a refuge in case of danger. It was a position of exceptional strategic importance, and if Corinth levied heavy duty upon goods passing across the isthmus, she was also one of the most important maritime powers of the age. As early as the 8th century B.C., the Corinthians founded several colonies: Corcyra (Corfu), Syracuse, and Potidaea which were to prove to be the first foundations of her commercial power. From 657 onwards, under the rule of the Cypselides, Corinth flourished, not only by trading, but also through the production of purple dye, carpets, painted vases and artistic bronzes. From 437 onwards the prosperity of Corinth dwindled for a while because of a series of wars with Athens, but from 350 to 146 the Corinthians regained their prosperity by profiting from the misfortunes of Athens, until the coming of the Romans who captured the city, plundered it and destroyed it.

In the year 44 B.C., Julius Caesar founded a new city on the site of the ancient one, but in A.D. 267 it was stormed by the Heruls and, after further attacks during successive centuries, there was a gradual decline.

After passing through the remains of a market of the Imperial era, we reach the site of major excavations, beginning first of all with the *Temple of Apollo*, one of the most ancient and most celebrated in Greece. Built between 550 and 525 B.C., on the site of a 7th-century sanctuary, it stands on a rocky terrace which dominates the *agora*. Of the peristyle which had no less than 38 columns, 7 are still standing and supporting fragments of the architrave.

We will then continue on our way by the Lechaion which

was lined with Corinthian colonnades under which there were shops on the western side. On this side too there were monumental buildings: a market, a great basilica, whilst on the left there were baths, the peribolus of Apollo, and the Pirene Fountain. Two flights of steps led to the *agora* through some *propylaea* which were composed of a monumental triumphal arch of marble surmounted by the two great gilded bronze chariots of Phaeton and Heios built in the 1st century A.D.

The *agora* is a vast square with two lines of shops at the sides.

To the west of the *propylaea*, a monumental façade, called the *Monument of the Captive Barbarians*, Corinthian in style and on two storeys, was made up of four huge statues of captive barbarians, standing on plinths decorated in high relief, symbolizing the victories of the Roman armies. Fragments of this monument are displayed in the museum.

Further on, a supporting wall, dating perhaps from the 5th century B.C., is broken by a staircase leading to a subterranean room where there was a sacred fountain. Originally it must have been out in the open, and the water flowed from marble nozzles fitted with lions' heads, but the spring that fed it must have dried up at the beginning of the 3rd century B.C. This fountain was carefully surrounded by walls, and a basin, fed by streams diverted from the city, was built above.

Nearby a sanctuary used by oracles has been excavated from the ruins of shops of the Roman era. It must have been constructed in the 5th century B.C. around a small, still older altar near to which libations were made before consulting the oracle, and worshippers waited to hear the pronouncement of the gods. A priest used to crawl through a passage only wide enough for him to pass. By this means he arrived at a mobile metope which differed in no way from those next to it, and it was through this channel that he voiced the prophecies of the oracle.

Behind the ruins of the Roman shops there appear to be the vestiges of a north-western portico of the Hellenistic age and built in the 3rd century B.C. The outer colonnade was of the Doric Order whilst the inner columns, which are half as numerous, were Corinthian.

After passing in front of the *propylaea* once more, we must direct our footsteps towards the Lower Pirene Spring which was used from the remotest ages until the end of the 19th century. By descending into the courtyard laid out in the 2nd century A.D. by Herodes Atticus, we shall find six basins communicating with a large subterranean reservoir fed by two springs with an average output of a cubic metre an hour, even in summer. The sides of a third basin are decorated with paintings of fish of the Roman Era. Pillars forming a portico supported the rocky vaulting. Later on, this portico was divided into six chambers separated by partitions, on which traces of Roman paintings can still be seen.

At the far end of the *agora*, lie the ruins of the *Julian Basilica*, built in the reign of Augustus, and several statues of emperors and members of the Julian family have been transported from this church to the museum containing objects found in the excavations of Corinth.

Further on to the west is to be found part of the pavement of the Greek *agora* below the level of the Roman pavement. Here, excavations have laid bare a line of blocks of poros covered with stucco, which marked the starting point of the Greek stadium. Holes were hollowed out in these blocks in which athletes thrust their toes in order to launch themselves more vigorously into the track. A second starting point, beyond this first one, is older and traces of wheels lead one to believe that this stadium was also used for chariot racing.

To the south a curved wall supported a terrace from which spectators and referees watched the racing.

Two rows of fifteen shops were on each side of the lower *agora* on which was the *Bema*, the monumental gallery on which the Roman governor presented himself to the citizens. It has been compared to the Rostrum, the speakers' tribune of ancient Rome, and it was from here in Corinth that St. Paul appeared before the Roman Governor Gallio to make a speech to defend himself and the Christian faith.

A building to the south of the Julian basilica was perhaps the *Tabularium* which housed the archives of the city. In front of the southern portico there was a terrace with a supporting wall which was discovered beneath the marble pavement of Roman times. On this terrace there were about 100 statues which were carried off to Italy after the sack of Corinth in A.D. 146.

The southern portico was one of the largest buildings of ancient Greece. Built in the 4th century B.C. and restored two centuries later, shortly before the destruction of the city by Mummius, it comprised in its southern sector two rows of 33 shops which were, for the most part, taverns. All the shops of the first row save two had wells 12 metres deep which were supplied with fresh water by a conduit linked with the Pirene Spring. These wells also served to cool food and drink. Thus, pitchers, goblets, cups, marble tables and tiles as well as other objects were thrown into these wells at the time of the plunder of the city. With these tiles, the roof of a part of the portico has been reconstructed under the shed which protects a Roman mosaic.

This curious building was part of a hostelry constructed to house the delegates of the Greek city-states at the time of the Pan Hellenic League. The floor which extended over the taverns was reserved for the lodging of these visitors.

The portico was completely rebuilt during the Roman domination, then, in the 1st century, the shops were pulled down and replaced by administrative offices.

It is possible to recognize two large halls in ruins, and then a third, with Roman mosaics protected by a shed, which must have been used for meetings of the *agonothetes* who were the judges at the Isthmic Games. The central panel represented a victorious athlete wearing a laurel wreath and standing in front of Tyche, the goddess of Fortune, whom he appeared to thank.

A second shed affords protection to two mosaic pavements, of which one represents Dionysus on a chariot drawn by panthers and led by a satyr holding a *thyrsus*, as well as two Centaurs with vases in their hands. The second mosaic represents a Nereid seated on the crupper of a Centaur, and Eros flying through the air.

In the fourth hall, a statue dedicated to a procurator of Trajan has been discovered. After this there was a passage leading to a marble staircase giving access to the *Southern Basilica*, a vast construction with an interior courtyard surrounded by porticoes from which the mutilated statues of several emperors have been taken.

Further on appear the ruins of a marble Roman fountain with the ground still covered with slabs of marble of different colours; then, just before the Senate, there is a passage to the road to Kenchreae, one of the two ports of Corinth. Under the Senate and the *Bema*, excavators have discovered the necropolis of the end of the Geometric period, with its ditches closed with slabs of stone, and a little subterranean chapel.

Besides several shops, we should note a great building and some Roman baths, the ruins of six little Roman temples, and of a foundation which supported a circular monument of Corinthian style built at the expense of the magistrate Babbius Philenus. Parallel to this line of temples were two rows of shops separated by a monumental stairway leading to an esplanade. Some of these shops are still in a fair state of preservation. In front of them was a composite Corinthian colonnade where the effigies of griffins, sirens, winged lions and human beings figured next to each other, together with scrolls of acanthus leaves.

After this, we will wend our way towards the high substructure of a temple which may be the one dedicated to Octavius referred to by Pausanias.

Near this temple is the museum containing most of the interesting pieces found during the excavation of the *agora* of Corinth or the surrounding region.

On the way to the exit of the excavation site can be seen the ruins of a temple dedicated perhaps to Hera Acraia, and which was built during the Roman domination.

In the vicinity, the *Fountain of Glauke*, set in an enormous square block of rock, took its name from the daughter of King Creon, second wife of Jason, chief of the Argonauts, who threw herself into the water to alleviate the terrible burns caused by the nuptial robes offered to her by Medea the witch, who had been abandoned by Jason. The Fountain comprised four reservoirs and could be reached through a portico of three columns flanked by altars and supporting an elliptical vault which has now collapsed. It was restored by the Romans but was converted into a house in the Middle Ages.

A second field of excavations is dedicated to the Odeon and to the theatre. The *cavea* of the odeon can still be seen, and it held about 3,000 spectators. It was built in the 1st century A.D., rebuilt at the expense of Herodes Atticus towards 175, and transformed in 225 into an arena where gladiatorial combats were held.

The *theatre*, built in the 5th century B.C., was entirely reconstructed by the Romans, and later adapted for nautical displays. The Greek auditorium is better preserved than the Roman auditorium. The wall of the Roman period, separating the auditorium from the orchestra, was adorned with paintings representing gladiatorial combats and combats of wild animals. A very simple inscription recalls the touching story of Androcles and the Lion.

Four hundred metres away, the ruins of the *Asclepieion* and the *Fountain of Lerne* were frequented by the sick who also consulted the god of healing in the neighbouring sanctuary.

The temple, built in the 4th century B.C. on the edge of a natural terrace at the foot of the ramparts, was surrounded by a wall with an interior colonnade with foundations which can still be distinguished. It is also possible to discern the plan of the temple which included a huge room, or *abaton*, where patients spent the night in the hope that the gods would suggest to them in their dreams the right remedy for their malady. A stairway led to the fountain composed of a large edifice with a central courtyard surrounded on all sides by colonnades. There was access to the basins of healing waters in the southern and the south-western galleries. The three rooms opened on to the colonnades, and situated as they were, under the *abaton*, they were used as dining-rooms with stone benches where patients sat and ate their food on small tables.

On leaving these excavations we go on to ACROCORINTH, with fortifications dating mainly from the 4th century B.C. The ramparts were restored in the reign of Justinian, shortly before the Slav invasion of 583. The garrison repelled the Bulgars in 981 and 985, and it was at about this time that the Byzantines added new fortifications to the citadel. In 1210, after a siege lasting five years, the Franks succeeded in capturing it. The fortifications were then reinforced once more, and Acrocorinth became a fief of the Villehardouins and then of the Angevins.

Many times captured and recaptured later on, the Castle had three rings of ramparts. The first was surrounded by a dry moat carved out of the rock by the Venetians, and then pierced with a gateway by the Franks. The second wall is partly of Byzantine origin with a curtain wall completed in the 15th century by the Knights of Rhodes. The third wall is reinforced with powerful rectangular towers, built mainly by the Byzantines, yet there are strips of masonry of the 4th century B.C.

Within the walls, we must note the ruins of a two-storeyed keep built most probably during the Frankish régime by

Guillaume de Villehardouin. Near the highest part of the hill is the substructure of the celebrated Temple of Artemis.

On the way back to the Athens highway, the Isthmia road leads to the ruins of the ancient sanctuary of Poseidon, god of the Isthmus, and 400 metres from a fortress erected by Justinian. Every two years in the spring, from 582 B.C. onwards, the games that were celebrated here were the most important in Greece after those of Olympia. According to legend they were initiated by Poseidon, or perhaps by Sisyphus, to commemorate the death of the oriental hero Melikertes, known also as Palemon, the Wrestler.

Nothing remains except the foundations of the temple built in the 5th century B.C. on the site of an Archaic temple destroyed in 475 B.C. by a tempest. Repaired several times during the Roman domination, it was pulled down by Justinian and the material was used for the construction of the ramparts erected to bar the passage of the Isthmus.

Between the temple and the modern road can be seen the line of the starting point of the Greek stadium of the Isthmus, formed by a triangular pavement, formerly covered by a layer of clay. Sixteen channels fan out from a central well, one metre deep. At each extremity of these channels are set up bronze horsemen sealed with lead. At the base of the triangles we can see the holes made for the insertion of vertical posts. A referee, seated in the well, could make the barriers fall down by tugging at a rope, thus giving the runners the starting signal. The bronze horsemen were used to keep the ropes in place for the different races.

In this region there are also the ruins of a 4th-century theatre which was rebuilt in the 1st century A.D. and, near to it, are the ruins of the Byzantine castle erected by Justinian with masonry taken from the fortifications constructed in the 5th century at the time of the Persian invasions.

Finally, the port of HERAION OF PERACHORA can be visited by passing through Loutraki and Perachora. The small harbour is delightful, whilst in the vicinity are the ruins of a Doric portico, the vestiges of a high altar, and those of a Temple of Hera Acriaia of the third quarter of the 6th century B.C. which replaced one of the Geometric period. Little remains of the *agora* of the 5th century and only the foundations of another Temple of Hera Limenia.

We continue towards Mycenae across the plain to the south and see Mount Daphnias crowned by a medieval fortress, and to the north, the territory of the ancient city of *Claenea*, an ally of Argos which still has the remains of a polygonal ring of ramparts and of some buildings on a hill.

Beyond the station of Nemea, a road to the right leads to the site of ancient *NEMEA* with the ruins of a temple dedicated to Zeus. Nemea was celebrated as the place where Hercules overcame the lion which terrorized the local population. The Nemean Games were one of the four great panhellenic festivals and were celebrated every two years under the auspices of Cleonae or of Argos.

The Temple of Zeus was a peripteral Doric temple of the 4th century B.C. and contemporary of the Temple of Tegea. Three columns in the middle of the vineyards still support a fragment of the entablature. Others have fallen, and one could wish that they could be set up again. In the interior of the temple a stairway led to the crypt or *adyton*.

The *sphendone* of the stadium has been found near a grotto which the peasants believe to have been the lion's lair. At the side is a rock shaped like an animal, and it is perhaps this malformation which has inspired the legend of the Lion of Nemea.

Returning to the highway and continuing towards Phychtia, a road to the left leads to the village of Mycenae, the site of much development in preparation for it becoming a tourist centre of the future.

A restaurant lunch will provide us with a bottle of the local red wine, a noble vintage suitably named *Le Sang d'Hercules* with its label showing the hero struggling against the Nemean lion. Thus fortified, we can explore the remains of antiquity that lie in front of us.

Beyond the fork that branches off to the Pavilion of Tourism, the road passes near some Mycenaean tombs carved out of the rock, then runs along the supporting wall of the terrace of the most imposing Mycenaean sepulchre, the one which is known as the Treasury of Atreus or Tomb of Agamemnon. Then the impressive acropolis of *MYCENAE* comes into view.

This acropolis was occupied from the beginning of the Bronze Age, towards 3,000 B.C. According to tradition, the Palasgians of the plain were first of all dominated by Danaos who had come from Egypt, while Acrisios reigned at Argos. Shortly afterwards, the brother of Danaos, Proestos, founded Tiryns, and Perseus, grandson of Acrisios, founded Mycenae on his return from long, protracted expeditions in Asia with the Cyclops. The dynasty of Perseus disappeared when the Achaians, led by Pelopides, came from Elis and settled in the Peloponnesus. Mycenae then became the capital of a powerful kingdom.

The arrival of the Achaians is estimated to have been about the year 2,000 B.C. at the beginning of the Middle Bronze Age which came to an end towards 1600 B.C. and, judging by the numerous gold objects found in the royal tombs, Mycenae must have been a very prosperous city and in close relationship with Crete.

After having discovered what he believed to be the treasury of Priam, Schliemann came to Mycenae, still bent on pursuing the footsteps of the heroes of Homer. He was haunted by the memory of Agamemnon returning to Mycenae the "golden" and his assassination in his bath by Queen Clytemnestra and her lover, Aegysthus, according to one version, and in the course of a banquet with all his companions according to another. Already in the time of Pausanias, all that remained of the ruined town were the Cyclopean walls and the tombs shaped like beehives which were sometimes visited by Greek or Roman travellers. One phrase from the works of Pausanias had impressed Schliemann: "Clytemnestra and Aegysthus were buried outside the walls, for they were not considered to be worthy of interment inside the city where lay the ashes of Agamemnon and his companions."

As he was not interested in the tombs of *tholos* in the valley, since they had been plundered and explored so many times in the past, he began to dig within the confines of the citadel behind the Lion Gate, and it is there that he discovered a collection of tombs in the shape of vertical wells, in the bottom of which he discovered the remains of nineteen people, and a number of precious objects. The men had their faces covered with masks of gold, and plaques of gold on their breasts, while the women wore golden diadems or tiaras. He was convinced that he had found the remains of Agamemnon and his companions, though in fact they were the remains of still more ancient princes. Later on, the members of the royal family were buried in *tholos*, these great *hypogea* with circular chambers, of which the oldest, dubbed Cyclopean, dates from between 1510 and 1460 B.C. This change corresponds doubtless to the accession of a new dynasty which succeeded to the dynasty of the tombs, and was believed to have reigned for a century, and contemporary probably of the XVIIIth Egyptian dynasty. Towards the middle of the 14th century B.C. the citadel was enlarged and protected by a wall of Cyclopean stones. It was at that time that one of the two royal tombs was included within the *enceinte* and surrounded by a double line of *stele*.

The power and influence of Mycenae appear to have grown still greater in the 13th century B.C. when Agamemnon was the undisputed leader of the Achaian coalition against Troy. After Orestes had killed Clytemnestra to avenge the murder of his father, and had had to leave the Kingdom of Mycenae, a civil war broke out, and the lower city was burnt down.

Towards the end of the 12th century, the Doric invasion put an end to the domination of the Mycenaeans and their citadel and capital were also burnt down.

Henceforth Mycenae was nothing more than an unimportant country town. Nevertheless it continues to be for us the city that best evokes the Greece of Homer, of the legends, of the Trojan War provoked by the kidnapping of Helen as a pretext for an expedition in search of plunder.

From the esplanade where cars have to be left, a track leads to the entrance of the Acropolis. First of all, there is the outer royal *enceinte* dating from the 18th century B.C. and partly destroyed when the tomb of Clytemnestra was built.

It contained vertical tombs of the same type as those in the Acropolis. Eight tombs have been excavated, each one of them surmounted by a small tumulus supported by a ring of stones and situated for the most part within the walls.

A few yards away, the tomb known as the grave of Clytemnestra and built towards the year 1300 B.C., is entered by a passage leading to a door surmounted by three enormous lintels. The funerary chamber is 13 metres high and in a good state of preservation. The grave where a woman was buried is in the *dromos* (passage).

The slope of the hill where this tomb was made is hollowed out so as to make the tiers for the Hellenistic theatre. Some of the imprints of these tiers can be discerned in the *dromos*, whilst a few metres away there is a second sepulchre, known as the tomb of Aegysthus, built between 1510 and 1460 B.C., but less well-preserved.

Further along this track to the Acropolis we can see remains of a fountain which may be the Fountain of Perseus, mentioned by Pausanias. It is composed of two basins backing on to a wall of poros of the Classical period. The fountains themselves are of the Hellenistic era, but the conduit is of an earlier date.

Beyond this, a ramp passing between two bastions brings

us to the Lion Gate which no one can behold without emotion, for it recalls the entire tragedy of the Atrides in an impressive and barbaric fashion. These two wild animals, facing each other on either side, of an immense lintel, cannot fail to add realism to the sagas of Homer.

The gate goes through the Cyclopean wall erected towards 1350 and in which three different kinds of masonry used can be discerned. The oldest is made up of enormous blocks of chalk, roughly shaped and held in place by small stones and lumps of clay in the interstices. The Lion Gate and the northern postern were constructed a little later with carefully hewn and shaped blocks of conglomerate and were faced and set in a more or less regular fashion. In the 3rd century B.C. some portions of this structure were rebuilt with thickset polygonal masonry. The thickness of the wall varies between three metres and eight metres.

Beyond the gate, we come to a passage which must have been roofed and closed by another gate that has disappeared. A small recess on the left was probably used as a porter's lodge.

Next we come to a great irregular polygonal-shaped space, bounded on the left by a big Cyclopean wall, built at a later date to support the upper terrace. On the right there were dwellings, a granary and the royal tombs protected by a well-preserved circular wall 26·50 metres in diameter.

The Royal Circle of the Acropolis is made up of two lines of slabs of stone 1·50 metres high, placed upright and sunk into the ground. It existed before the six royal tombs that it encloses and must have been constructed when the old royal cemetery was incorporated into the fortified area when the Lion Gate was erected.

It is here that Schliemann and Stamakis found the six tombs in 1876. Beyond this point there are remains of dwellings, and in one of these was found the celebrated "Vase of the Warrior" which is now in the National Museum at Athens.

Likewise, under this same house were discovered 16 tombs of a prehistoric cemetery. There were some vestiges of the *House of the Ramp* which included a *megaron* and was at least two storeys high. Beyond are the ruins of the *South House* and the *House of the Citadel* which were connected by a double corridor and the *House of Tsounas* which contained a mysterious shrine.

This last is near the polygonal tower which was part of the rampart rebuilt in the 3rd century B.C.

From the Lion Gate, a wide ramp comes to an end at a Hellenistic building with four rooms. From there the *Royal Way* wound up the slopes of the Acropolis to the entrance of a palace which occupied a series of terraces on the summit of the hill. A few vestiges of this 14th-century B.C. edifice are sufficient to give us some conception of what it must have looked like.

A courtyard paved with small pebbles was bounded to the south by a monumental gateway of which practically nothing remains. Further south, a fairway formerly covered with cement leads to another court from which a narrow passage leads to the central courtyard of the palace which was surrounded by the principal apartments.

To the south, a single flight of a monumental staircase still exists, whilst to the west was the throne room and, to the east, a portico facing the hall of the *megaron*.

A hall in front of the throne room communicated with the upper landing of the main staircase. This part of the palace must have been rebuilt after a fire.

Of the great staircase which led to the main courtyard, there subsists a flight of 22 steps, from the top of which a second flight of steps of wood, parallel to the first flight, made up for the difference in level between the landing and the main courtyard. The building which sheltered this stairway has disappeared.

The portico of the *megaron* was paved with slabs of gypsum

which were imported from Crete. Two circular bases supported pillars of wood. At each extremity of the porch, in the alignment of columns, there appears to be the foundation of a stone pier.

The porch communicated with the hall by a door whose threshold remains. The ground was covered with a layer of painted stucco with a border of gypsum, and in the centre, a raised circular hearth was enclosed by four wooden columns on a stone base which supported the roof. Near to the hearth, the king had a chair on a kind of pedestal. A few traces of the frescoes that decorated the walls have been discovered. It is here that Clytemnestra caused a purple carpet to be laid when Agamemnon returned, and a little room on one side is perhaps the bathroom where he was assassinated.

From a hall facing the porch, a wooden staircase led to the rooms on the upper storey probably reserved for the servants.

At the summit of the Acropolis can be seen the foundations of a Mycenaean temple of the palace which was rebuilt and enlarged repeatedly.

The descent down the eastern slope of the citadel passes, on the right-hand side, the ruins of a pillared house, a carefully constructed little palace which presents certain analogies, as far as the *megaron* is concerned, with the Palace of Ulysses described by Homer. It is situated near a tower which is among the most characteristic of the Cyclopean ramparts.

Next comes the supporting wall which was the outer wall of the citadel of the 14th century, before the construction a century later of a salient. This salient took in the entrance of a vaulted underground passage passing along the northern front by following a natural fissure in the rock to gain a secret cistern supplied with water by the Perseus Spring at a depth of 12 metres. The stairway has a first flight of 16 steps and then, after a sharp turn, a second flight of 93 steps. This colossal work, which dates from the 13th century B.C., was intended to ensure a supply of drinking water in the eventuality of a siege. Two narrow posterns were cut in the wall of the building.

By following the northern rampart in the direction of the Lion Gate, we will come upon a postern with an outer ramp contained between two bastions, and 100 metres further on, an inner gallery built on to the Cyclopean rampart.

On leaving the Acropolis and passing the second Royal Circle, there are, to the left of the road, remains of Mycenaean houses. First of all, we see the *House of the Bucklers* where a number of bilobed shields have been found, then a house of five rooms with a kitchen and terraces on a higher level. Next came the house of an oil merchant of the 13th century B.C., where a store contained 32 handled jars, of which some have kept their stamped clay stoppers though the vessels were destroyed by fire. Thirty-nine clay tablets were also discovered, as well as frescoes of an earlier building.

Further to the south, the so-called *House of the Sphinxes* of the 13th century B.C., is of a slightly later date. In it have been recovered two sphinxes, some ivory figures and some little Mycenaean columns, reduced models of the Goddess Column of the Lion Gate.

Finally 500 metres from the Acropolis we must visit the tomb, known as the *Tomb of Agamemnon* or the *Treasury of Atreus*, which we passed on our way up.

It is one of the most extraordinary monuments in the whole of Greece. It is reached by a deep trench whose sides are lined with carefully-hewn and disposed stones, which frame the entrance of the tomb with a triangular opening above a stone lintel weighing 120 tons.

The *tholos* is shaped like a beehive 13 metres high and 14½ metres in diameter. The cupola is formed of 33 superimposed, corbelled rings surmounted by a round slab that serves as a keystone. The upper part of the exterior is covered with clay to make the tomb waterproof. A passage leads to an inner room where a ditch has been carved out of the rock.

This particular tomb is the best-preserved, but there are several similar ones in the vicinity. Pausanias and other authors of Antiquity called these *tholos* treasure houses, and believed that it was there that the kings of old kept their wealth. However, as other similar chambers have been discovered in different parts of Greece, we know now that these sepulchres served the same purpose as the Pyramids of Egypt.

We will now return to the main road that follows, first of all, the Gorge of the Inachos and then that of the Xerias, and finally we arrive at ARGOS, the land of beautiful women or, in the words of Homer: "Argos with the rearing horses."

The little white houses of the town extend over the site of the ancient city which is dominated by two hills of which the one called Kastro is crowned by a Turkish fortress.

Argos (the Plain) was first of all inhabited by the Pelasgi and by King Phoroneus, founder of the Acropolis of Larissa (the Kastro), and then by the Danaeans. The legends of Perseus and of the seduction of his mother, Danae, by Zeus belong to this period. During the Mycenaean age, Argos was at its apogee. The Argolids participated in the expedition of the Seven against Thebes in the 13th century B.C. and then in the Trojan War. Orestes extended his dominion over Laconia and Acadia. After the invasion of the Peloponnesus by the Dorians, Argos fell to the Heraclide Temenus who became ruler of many of the other Dorian cities of Argolis. Argos was victorious in the wars against Sparta, but was beaten by Cleomenes I, King of Sparta, towards the year 540 and again in 520 when she lost 6,000 men and survived only because of the heroism of the poetess Telesilla. Recovering, Argos destroyed Mycenae and Tiryns and, towards the year 400, the city took on a democratic constitution and participated in various coalitions. Centuries later, Argos was ravaged by the Goths, but the city continued its existence.

The excavations of the French School of Athens have

brought to light several of the monuments of this city which is considered to be the most ancient in Greece.

The museum near the central square contains many of the most interesting objects found on this site, including some splendid paleo-Christian mosaics.

If we take the Tripolis road we will come upon the *agora* with an area limited by the houses huddled around it. Pausanias declares that 18 temples faced the square, but only a few vestiges of these monuments remain. There are however the ruins of a long Greek 5th-century B.C. building with interior colonnades which may have been the Senate of Argos, as well as of a colonnade which was reconstructed in the 4th century B.C. These two buildings were restored after the Gothic invasion of the year A.D. 396.

Beyond the *agora* in the excavation site between the foot of Larissa Hill and the Tripolis road, the Roman baths were built in the 2nd century A.D. and were restored two centuries later. The large entrance hall with a crypt contained three sarcophagi and communicated with a second hall with a broad transversal passage which may have been the changing room. Next came the *frigidarium* where one of the three piscina that it held still remains. Another passage also communicated with two *caldaria* built up on piles of bricks above the furnaces and which also had several piscina. The piscina of a third *caldarium* was lined with marble.

The theatre, disposed on the slope of hill, had 91 tiers of seats cut out of the rocks and was larger than the theatres of Athens or of Epidaurus, for it could accommodate 20,000 spectators. It was founded towards the end of the 4th century B.C. but had been remodelled twice during the Roman period, first in the 2nd century A.D. and then in the 4th century, at a time when the orchestra pit was replaced by a large tank for naval combats.

On the southern *parados*, there is a small bas-relief of the Dioscuri.

The orchestra, carved for the greater part out of the solid rock, is 26 metres in diameter. In the centre, a symbolic circle of thin slabs of stone dates from the Hellenistic theatre. Towards the end of the 5th century A.D., the ground was paved with blue and white marble so as to prevent the leakage of the basins which were supplied with water by a Roman aqueduct of the 3rd century A.D.

The foundations of the Greek stage remain. It comprised a proscenium with a colonnade, a wall backstage and a Doric portico. It was pulled down and replaced by a Roman stage which was built of brick faced with marble, and was remodelled in the 4th century A.D.

The first tier of the auditorium was just above the orchestra and was reserved for guests of honour who were accommodated on seats with comfortable backs.

On the way to the odeon nearby are the remains of a small Roman aqueduct. The odeon, a semi-circular assembly hall, was built by the Romans in the 1st century A.D. and remodelled two centuries later. It must have been erected on the site of a theatre with tiers, which probably served as an assembly room before the 4th century B.C.

The *kastro* on the hill was of Byzantine and Frankish construction, but was fortified and enlarged later on by the Turks.

It is composed of an elliptical ring of ramparts flanked with towers and a central keep with battlemented walls. The fortifications of the Acropolis must also have had two rings of ramparts, of which fragments are incorporated in the walls of the Kastro. The first wall dates from the 6th century B.C. and was strengthened on the outside by a Hellenic wall, of which vestiges can still be seen.

In the courtyard of the castle have been discovered the remains of two temples dedicated respectively to Zeus Larisaios and to Athena Polias.

The Acropolis of Larissa was linked up to the walls of the

city which extended as far as the Hill of Aspis whose summit was also crowned with a fortress.

Worthy of note also is a bas-relief carved out of the rock representing a horseman and a snake, a Mycenaean necropolis and the site of the Sanctuary of Apollo and Athena.

Then, on the summit of the hill of Haghios Hias, corresponding to the ancient Aspi (the Shield) there are the remains of a Hellenistic fortress built on the vestiges of the prehistoric Cyclopean wall. It forms, to the north-east, a triangular salient with two square towers and four posterns.

Heraion of Argos is only 9 kilometres from the city of Argos. At Chonika at the 7th kilometre, the beautiful church of the 11th century resembles the church of Merbaka but is older.

The HERAION OF ARGOS, the national sanctuary of Argos, was dedicated to Hera, and its ruins are situated on a rocky spur detached from Mount Euboia which dominates the Plain of Argolis.

The sanctuary lay between two streams: the Eutherios, whose waters were used for the purification of the priestesses, and the Asterion.

According to a legend, Cleobis and Biton were dragging the chariot of their mother, priestess of Hera, on the road from Argos to Heraion, but when they reached the sanctuary they fell asleep, never to wake again. It is also at Heraion that Agamemnon received the oath of allegiance of the Achaian chieftains before their departure for Troy. The primitive temple of the beginning of the 7th century B.C. was destroyed by fire in 423 because of the negligence of a priestess. The new temple was built a little lower down the slope by the Argian architect, Eupolemos.

Higher up can be seen a little edifice with square foundations and the remains of the new temple. The *cella* contained the chryselephantine statue of Hera, represented seated, and the work of Polycletus, as well as a *xoanon* of the goddess taken away from Tiryns by the Argolids in 468. Excavations have brought to light some fine sculptured façades representing the Birth of Zeus, the War of the Giants on one side, and the Capture of Troy on the other, as well as *metopes* representing warriors and Amazons, and fragments of the cornice.

The walls of different buildings and the huge understructure of the ancient temple have been cleared from the rubble.

Returning to Chonika, the road will lead us to MERBAKA, a small village, where there is one of the most beautiful churches in Argolis. It is dedicated to *Panaghia* and dates from the 12th century, but was remodelled in the 15th and 16th centuries. It is planned on the lines of a Greek cross, like the churches of the 10th and 11th centuries in Athens. The dome reposes on four slender columns of green marble. The capitals are decorated in a pattern of acanthus leaves. The inner decoration of the walls with brick is of exceptional artistic quality and so are the three triple-arched windows. Plaques of ceramics adorn the walls. There are fine marble ornaments and a sundial, also of marble. It was probably the church of a monastery.

From Merbaka a track leads to Dendra, a hamlet from which one can go on foot to the rocky peak of Dendra, crowned by the Acropolis of MIDEA, founded by Perseus and birthplace of Alcmene, mother of Hercules.

The Cyclopean ring of walls is of the same pattern as the *enceinte* of Tiryns and forms a half-circle on the western slope which links up with the ridge above a ravine. On the northern front, the stonework is better preserved, for it is still from 6 to 7 metres high.

Two hundred metres from the village, a Mycenaean necropolis has been discovered and, in a vault, a bronze breastplate together with the whole panoply of a Mycenaean warrior: a helmet with wild boar's teeth and metal cheek plates, all of them answering completely to the descriptions of Homer.

From Merbaka we go to *TIRYNS* with its Acropolis on

the summit of a rocky hillock. The walls of Tiryns are even more impressive than those of Mycenae, for did not Homer write of "Tiryns with its ramparts"?

Indeed we will find most of the heroes of Greek mythology in its legendary history. Founded by Proestos, brother of Acrision, King of Argos, with the help of some Cyclops whom he had sent for from Lycia, it was then governed by Perseus, Amphitryon and Eurystheus. It is this Eurystheus who imposed the twelve labours on Hercules so that he could purify himself of the crime of having caused the death of his children by Megara, and also in the hope of ridding himself of this embarrassing servitude.

The Acropolis of Tiryns had been inhabited since the third millennium B.C. A circular palace existed on the summit and the periphery of the hall was fortified at a very early date, but it was towards the year 1400 that the Cyclopean walls were constructed. The latter were restored repeatedly, more especially in the year 1200 B.C., when the palace whose ruins can still be seen, was built.

After a walk along the western side of the fortress, a road on the left, and then a path, provide access to the gateway which is preceded by a ramp with a width of 4·70 metres that can be used by chariots.

The fortified perimeter is an oblong 300 metres long by 160 metres wide. The wall is constructed of Cyclopean blocks, each of which has been roughly hammered into shape and weighs 13 tons. Certain parts have been more evenly constructed with facings and are more closely set. The thickness of the walls varies from 7 to 10 metres.

After having passed through the principal gate, we have to turn left for the upper terrace of the Acropolis where stood the royal palace within its own *enceinte*.

Within 17 metres of the gate, in a passage between the outer and inner walls, was the door of the upper terrace which was probably like the Lion Gate of Mycenae, for it has the same dimensions. In the monolithic threshold, we can see holes for the staples of the hinges and, in the jambs on each side, the holes in which was fitted an iron bar to close the door. The terrace was lined with a kind of wooden loggia, built above a gallery and casemates which were used as storehouses.

To the right, the Great Propylaeum, with a threshold made of a single slab of blue stone, was the principal entrance of the *gynaeceum.*

The Great Propylaeum led into a courtyard surrounded on three sides by the ramparts and, on the fourth, by the palace. Opposite, a covered gallery and five casemates are merged into the wall. They were reached by passing under a portico and by descending a covered staircase which is still discernible, with its right-angled turning. It came to an end at a gallery 20 metres long with a floor 7 metres below the terrace. To the right, a narrow arrow slit has been cut out in the thickness of the rampart. Further on, a rectangular bastion contained two cisterns with slate roofs.

Returning to the main courtyard, we have to cross a second *propylaeum*, smaller than the first, which opened out on to another court with a cemented floor, and there remains nothing of the palace save the foundations. To the right of the entrance, the hollow of a massive square of masonry in the centre marks the royal altar with its ditch for sacrifices. The eastern and western sides of the courtyard were lined with porticoes and rooms reserved for guests and their servants. Opposite the *propylaeum* there was a portico in the façade of the main body of the palace and there was a hall in front of the *megaron* in the centre of which the fireplace was surrounded by four wooden columns that supported the ceiling.

By walking along the west front of the *enceinte*, we come upon the entrance of a well-preserved secret passage with a stairway made in the stonework of the ramps. It leads to a vaulted postern gate through which we may pass.

Next we proceed to NAUPLIA, a charming little town on the Gulf of Argolis which lies at the foot of a rocky spur of the surrounding mountains, crowned by a mighty fortress and named after Palamedes who is said to have invented the games of chess and of dicing to distract the Achaeans during the Siege of Troy.

Originally independent, and then affiliated to the maritime league of Calaurea in 628 B.C., Nauplia was annexed by Argos and became the port and arsenal of Argolis. After having been under Byzantine domination until 1210, Nauplia was captured by the Franks under Guillaume de Villehardouin and became the fief of Guy de la Roche in 1277. The last of these Frankish lords placed the city under the protection of the Venetians who renamed it Napoli de Romania. The Turks besieged the city without success in 1500 and 1537, but the town was stormed in 1540 and became the capital of the province of Morea. The Venetian, Morosini, recaptured it in 1686 and installed a garrison there which remained until the Turkish reconquest in 1715. At the beginning of the War of Independence in the 19th century, Nauplia became the capital of liberated Greece.

On entering the city, the visitor will see, in Nikitara Square, to be precise, in the courtyard of a garage, a bastion of the Venetian citadel of Acronauplia, built in 1706 and dominated by a powerful outwork with two towers, also Venetian, but built at the end of the 15th or beginning of the 16th century.

This outwork was part of the ramparts built by the Venetians to the east of the Frankish wall at the time of the siege of 1205–1210. Further to the west, are the slight remains of another wall built by the Byzantines, before the Frankish conquest, on the top of fortifications of the Classical Age. A thick supporting embankment was erected between the Byzantine and the Frankish walls with embrasures for artillery. Towards 1701, a half-bastion was constructed to strengthen the defences of the northern front of the Byzantine castle. The monumental entrance gate made in this half-bastion was added in 1715 by the Venetians by a governor named Sagredo.

Vasileos Constantinou Street leads to the Syntagma Square which is lined with old houses, and it is here that we find the museum installed in a building used by the Venetians as barracks. In the interior there is a splendid collection of vases from Mycenae and Tiryns as well as of many other objects found in the course of excavations, by the English School of Athens.

In one corner of the Square, the Vouleftiko, a former mosque, was the seat of the first Assembly of Liberated Greece. Another mosque, also in this square, has been transformed into a theatre.

Further on, in another square on the quayside, a monument of marble was erected in 1903 in memory of Marshal Maison, General Fabrier, Admiral de Rigny and the French soldiers and sailors who died fighting for Greek Independence. From there and from the opposite mole, there is a view of the Burzi Islet, formerly linked to the mainland by a causeway, with a Venetian fortress which has been converted into an hotel.

By following a number of narrow lanes it is possible to visit the Citadel of Acronauplia. The Palamedes Citadel, which crowns a steep promontory, can be reached by climbing 875 steps to the 710 metres high rock on which it is situated, or alternatively by driving up the circular Leoforos 25-Martiou.

This last citadel was built for the Venetians in 1715 by the French Colonel La Salle who was commissioned to do so by the Governor Augustino Sagredo. It communicated with the fortress of Acronauplia by a secret passage, and had besides seven isolated towers. On the way up we shall find, perched on a rock and surrounded by cypresses, the *Church of Evangelistria.*

Incidentally, near the main square of the suburb of Pronia where the Assembly confirmed the election of Prince Otto as

King of the Hellenes in 1832, we can see an immense stone lion carved by Siegel in 1833.

Leaving Nauplia by the Epidaurus road, a track on the right leads to HAGHIA MONI, a convent founded in 1144 with its typically Byzantine Church of *Theotomotos*, also called *Zoodochos Pighi*, built four years later. It stands near the spring identified as the Canathos, a sacred rivulet where the goddess Hera bathed once a year to regain her virginity. In the vicinity there are remains of walls, of wells, and of an aqueduct.

If we continue by the road to Epidaurus, we shall find, 13 kilometres further on the left-hand side and 50 metres before crossing a ravine by a modern bridge, an ancient bridge of Cyclopean structure, which appears to date from the Classical period. The roadway, which crossed the river by this bridge, led to the Acropolis of Kasarmi, to be seen on the left. A ramp led to the principal gateway which is defended by a round tower. The wall, built of polygonal masonry of the 5th century B.C. was reinforced by round towers and, on the foundations of these structures, the Franks built their bastions. To the north, a Frankish tower with a staircase can be seen near an ancient postern.

Sixteen kilometres further on, the hillock of KASTRAKI is crowned by the ruins of another acropolis with an entrance protected by a square tower and still further strengthened by an interior gate protected by a round tower. The walls of fine polygonal stone are fortified by round and square towers.

Another 8 kilometres brings us to the church of HAGHIA MARINA, built on the site of a temple dedicated to Athena. Near the church are the remains of an Ionic structure and of a pyramid built in the 4th century B.C., which was perhaps a fortalice where a small garrison could take refuge in the event of a surprise attack. It was restored or modified repeatedly and remained in use until the 5th century A.D.

We must now return to the Epidaurus road, driving on to

the village of Ligourio where we will turn to the right to visit the sanctuary of Asclepios and the site of the ancient city of EPIDAURUS.

The sanctuary of Asclepios, the Aesculapius of the Romans, is the most celebrated of the places dedicated to the healing god. It is claimed that Asclepios was born not far from there on a mountain where he was fed by a goat. The cult of this god was introduced into the territory of Epidaurus towards the 6th century B.C., but it was only in the 4th century that it attained such fame and that most of the buildings, whose ruins we shall visit, were erected, as well as the great theatre which has been so wonderfully preserved.

According to legend, Phlegias, King of Orchomenus in Boeotia, came to Epidaurus on a war of conquest. Apollo seduced his daughter, Coronis, who gave birth to a child secretly on Mount Thittion. She died in bringing the child into the world, and so he was fed by a goat. Apollo entrusted the education of his son to the centaur Chiron who taught him the virtues of wild plants. A shepherd who gave shelter to the boy was astonished to see a halo round his brow, and the rumour spread that a god was born to heal the sick and even restore the dead to life, and this aroused the anger of Zeus.

The Hieron of Asclepios of Epidaurus became the most celebrated sanctuary of the god. Patients began by offering a first ritual sacrifice to Apollo, and their offerings were so lavish that they aroused the greed of pirates and even of Sulla who ordered the distribution of these gifts to his soldiers. During the Roman era, the priests assisted the miraculous cures by the exercise of medical practice and so they added baths and a sanatorium to the sanctuary.

After having walked along the stadium to the right and then through a vast field of ruins on the left, we come upon the theatre which is the largest and best preserved in the whole of Greece. It was built in the 4th century B.C. by an architect and sculptor of Argolis, named Polycletus the Younger, the distinguish him from the great sculptor of the preceding century. All that remains of the stage are the foundations and the orchestra where the choir stands in a great circle of beaten earth.

The acoustics are exceptionally good, and even from the most distant tiers one can hear the slightest sound made by someone standing in the centre of the orchestra on the spot where the altar once stood.

Around the orchestra the stalls with backs of red chalk were reserved for the magistrates and guests of note.

From the theatre it is possible to climb up to the ruins of the Temple of Apollo Maleatas which date from the 4th century B.C., but they are so insignificant that they need not be visited, and we can see instead some statues and fragments of sculpture in the museum before going on to the remains of the great sanctuary.

First of all there are the remains of a great square building which must have been the hotel, and those of a Greek bath which was an annex of the gymnasium. It was transformed into an odeon under the Romans, and the *propylaeum* was turned into a place of worship dedicated to Hygea. The gymnasium comprised a large interior courtyard with a peristyle and lined with rectangular *exedra* with columns inside, porticoes and rooms of different types and sizes.

To the north of the gymnasium are the ruins of a *palestra* and of the Colonnade of Cotys. After the *palestra* came the real sanctuary and the *peribolus* surrounding it was transformed into a fortress by the Byzantines.

After passing the remains of the substructure of a small temple of Themis, we shall come upon the vestigial ruins of a Roman building and of a temple of Artemis of the 4th century B.C.

Nearby there is a building which may be the former *abaton*, a vast dormitory where the patients slept on beds or on benches whilst waiting for the manifestation of the god who was to bring them healing during their slumbers.

In Hellenistic or Roman times, the building was connected to an altar by a paved pathway.

We now come to the Temple of Asclepios, built by the architect Theodore between 380 and 375 B.C., and all that remains of this edifice are the foundations and some fragments which can be inspected in the museum.

It was a Doric temple, peripteral and hexastyle, without an *opisthodome* and entirely built of Corinthian tufa, save for the carvings and the framework of the doors. In the *cella* and in a kind of well, the chryselephantine statue of Asclepios was the work of the sculptor Thrasymedes of Paros.

The *tholos* which stood to the west of the temple was one of the most remarkable examples of Greek architecture of the 4th century B.C. It was built between 360 and 330 to the plans of Polycletus the Younger who supervised the first phase of the construction. This building, called the Thymele or altar, has been the subject of a great deal of controversy.

All that remains are the foundations made up of six concentric circular walls of conglomerate. The three walls furthest from the centre were unbroken, but in the three inner walls, there were doors, and the walls themselves were separated from each other by partitions. Doors and partitions were so arranged that, to pass from one passage to another to go to the centre, it was necessary to walk almost round the passage that you wished to leave. Among the different conjectures that have been made about this kind of labyrinth, the most plausible is that it was used to house the sacred serpents of the sanctuary. According to Pausanias, these snakes, especially the pale coloured ones dedicated to Asclepios, never harm anyone. They belong to a species which is only found at Epidaurus.

To these details we must add that the exterior wall supported a colonnade, that the second wall was pierced by a door, and that the third wall had an inner colonnade. The outer colonnade had 26 Doric columns, the inner one had

14 Corinthian columns. Pausanias relates that in the interior there were paintings representing scenes of love and of drunkenness.

Beyond the *tholos* a line of porticoes was divided in the middle by a separating wall to create the *enkoimeterion* or *abaton* or secret portico which replaced an older building in the 4th century B.C. *Stele* describing miraculous cures are now in the museum.

At the eastern extremity, the curb of a well has been found which may have been part of a shrine used for some Archaic form of worship. Then there are the vestiges of a building identified as the Bath of Asclepios, constructed in the 2nd century A.D. by the Roman senator Antonius more or less on the top of an older building of the 5th century B.C.

From there we can proceed to the holy place, surrounded on three sides by the bases of columns and by an *exedra* with seats. Further on are the ruins of a vast portico with several galleries and a group of thermal constructions supplied with water by the springs and streams of Mount Kynortion.

After inspecting the ruins of the *propylaea* of the sanctuary constructed in tufa in the 4th century B.C., we can see, on our way back to the Stadium, the remains of a little temple dedicated to Aphrodite, those of a vast Hellenic cistern, then a rectangular well which must have been the fountain of the Stadium.

The Stadium, laid out in the 5th century B.C. in the hollow of a natural ravine, had some tiers carved out of the rock and others built of masonry.

On returning to Nauplia, we must first take the road to Argos. From Argos we go on towards Tripolis and, on leaving the village of Myli, we will note, on our left, a structure of concrete erected to protect the remains of the ancient city of *Lerna*, celebrated in Greek Mythology as the site of the combat between Hercules and the Hydra.

Although the ruins of Lerna are reduced to the foundations

of the building which composed it, they do deserve some attention. These vestigial remains date from the first occupation of this site in the Neolithic era (the 4th and 3rd millennia), to the Mycenaean Age (between 1600 and 1200 B.C.).

If we leave on the left the building which protects the most interesting ruins, we will find first of all the remains of a rampart reinforced by towers and dating from the beginning of the 3rd millennium. These were modified several times during that period. Then, in a ditch, there are the vestiges of a Neolithic house.

Further on amid the remains of fortifications of the Ancient Helladic Age, we shall see the traces of a staircase and of two towers, still of the Ancient Helladic Age. Under a modern roof, a strip of unbaked bricks is next to the foundations of two absidial houses almost superimposed on each other, and dating from the mid-Helladic Age (2000–1600 B.C.).

Amongst the substructure of houses of this period, one appears to have been a shop and another a kitchen.

Besides these discoveries there are also the remains of what may have been the first palace which preceded the House of the Tiles. Dating from the Ancient Helladic Age, it consisted of a one-floor dwelling with walls covered with stucco chiselled in decorative designs. Two tombs were dug here, the first towards the end of the Middle Helladic Age, the second at the beginning of the Mycenaean Age. The remains of the House of the Tiles, after it was ravaged by a fire, were partly used in the arrangement of a circular floor lined at the edges with big pebbles, where *bothroi* (hollow sacrificial altars) were dug.

From here we go on to TRIPOLIS, a little town of relatively recent foundation, which is of no interest save for the fact that it has hotels and restaurants.

Now we must return to Sparta on our way to Monemvasia. If the state of the road is not too bad, we should go through

Geraki, but we could previously have turned off to CHRYSAPHA which is 18 kilometres away. Here we shall find several interesting Byzantine churches, including more especially the *Chrysaphiotissa*, built in 1290, which has some frescoes; so has the Church of All Saints (formerly the Church of the Podrome) where the *Assumption of the Virgin* is really remarkable. We must also visit the *Church of the Dormition and S. Demetrios* which date only from the 17th century. A little to one side, the *Church of the Monastery of the Prodome* was founded in 1625, and is not devoid of interest. The monastery of the Forty Martyrs between Sparta and Chrysapha, but some way off from the road, has a church carved out of the rock with 14th-century frescoes.

GERAKI, the *Geronthrae* of the Ancients, is a big village where we may visit the Church of the Evanghelios with rather faded frescoes, the Haghios Youmis near the fountain and the Haghios Sozon which appears to be of the 12th century and is built on the plan of a Greek cross.

The village lies on the south slope of a hill whose summit is surrounded by the remains of a Pelasgic wall dating from the Bronze Age, but completed by the Franks, the Byzantines or the Venetians. However, apart from its medieval churches, the principal interest in Geraki lies in its Frankish Castle built in 1254 by Guy de Nevelet, Baron of Tsaconis. To get there, we must take the Haghios Dimitros road, leaving on the left the cemetery which has a few Byzantine frescoes, and continuing 500 metres further on by a rough track.

Before going on to Sparta, we should see the remains of *TEGEA* which was the most important city of the Upper Arcadian Plain and was, under the Franks, the seat of a rich Bishopric known as Nicli. The modern village is called PALEO EPISCOPI and, in front of a basilica of recent construction, there were some fine Paleochristian mosaics representing the twelve months of the year, allegorical figures of the Tigris and Euphrates, marine animals and an inscription mentioning the name of the bishop responsible for the building of the Byzantine Church. This was on the site of the present basilica. These mosaics have been removed to the Agricultural College of Tegea.

Tegea, the Protectorate, consisted originally of nine demes which Aleos, son of Apheidas, united into a single administration. This state defended the independence of Arcadia against the Dorians of Laconia, as we know from the duel between the Tegeat King Echemos with the Heraclide Hylos. Towards 550 B.C., Tegea accepted the overlordship of Sparta, and after the Battle of Leuctres (371) it joined a new Arcadian League. It was still flourishing in the time of Strabo and Pausanias, but was destroyed in the 4th century A.D. by Alaric. Repopulated by the Byzantines, under the Frankish domination, Tegea became one of the strongest towns in the Morea. In 1209 Geoffroy de Villehardouin set up a Barony there, which disappeared after the capture of the city by the Byzantines.

The antique city was built in the plain and surrounded an oval *enceinte* 5,500 metres in circumference. These ramparts were constructed of unfired bricks resting on a foundation of masonry. The celebrated Temple of Alea Athena was founded in the 9th century B.C. by King Aleos, and it was situated about 2 kilometres from the Basilica. It was a famous place of asylum, and both Orestes and Pausanias, King of Sparta, sought refuge there.

Important foundations of this ancient city still subsist near to the little village of Tegea. The Archaic temple, burnt down in 395–394 B.C., was rebuilt and decorated by the sculptor Scopas to serve as a setting for the ivory statue of Athena by the sculptor Endoios, and the remains of the wild boar of Calydon who was hunted and killed by Meleager and Atalanta. In front of the temple are vestiges of the altar which was decorated by the same sculptor. An ancient well to the right is said to be the one where Hercules raped Augia, priestess of Athena and mother of Telephus.

The Temple of Alea Athena was one of the most splendid of the Peloponnesus and also a religious centre of the Arcadian Confederation. It was a Doric peripteral temple with 6 columns on the façade and 14 columns on each side, but the columns of the *pronaos* were Doric and those of the *cella* were Corinthian: all of them were constructed on a foundation of tufa. Fragments of the pediments are on display at the local museum and in Athens.

The museum contains some fragments of carvings from the Temple, some mouldings and some original works of Scopas, including more especially the torso of the Nymph Hagnô, the federal altar of Tegea, as well as geometric ceramics and votive bronzes.

From Tegea it is best to rejoin the Sparta road directly. This highway crosses the Laconian Plain which is surrounded by the mountain ranges of Parnon and Taygetus. They transform this valley into a kind of fortress which was known as the Lacedemonian Hollow.

Fifty kilometres on, we leave, on the right, a road to the village of Sellasia 2 kilometres away which is near to the site of the Battle of Sellasia where the Macedonians and the Archaeans destroyed a Spartan army in 220 B.C.

The remains of the Acropolis of *SELLASIA* are to be found on the summit of Mount Haghios Constantinos, and of these there are ruins of walls flanked by towers representing what is left of a ring of outer fortifications surrounding an inner *enceinte*.

After crossing the River Eurotas, 10 kilometres further on, the Acropolis of Sparta comes into view.

In the present day, SPARTA is nothing more than a clean little provincial town with a large square and wide avenues with a line of trees running down the centre.

The attraction here is the presence of the nearby Byzantine city of Mistra, for the ruins of Ancient Sparta are far from impressive. Moreover the traditional austerity of the Spartans prevented them from erecting buildings as sumptuous as those in other parts of Greece. Indeed, as Thucydides wrote: "If Lacedaemon were ever completely devastated and there only remained the foundations of its temples and public buildings, the posterity of a faraway future would find it difficult to believe that the might of Sparta was as great as its fame."

However, the scenery is not without a certain grandeur, since it has as a background the Taygetus range with its rugged peaks outlined against the sky, and its foothills of which one is crowned by the Frankish castle of the Villehardouins.

In considering Sparta, we must remember that it was the legislator, Lycurgus, who propounded the idea of a military oligarchy, ruled by two kings reigning for life in time of war: one of these would have to be a member of an ancient Achaean family. In times of peace the country was to be governed by a senate of thirty aristocrats.

From 756 onwards, there was an executive council of five magistrates known as *ephores*.

There were three classes of citizens: the true Spartans who were known as the Equals and descended from the Doric conquerors who lived from the profits of their lands which they did not cultivate themselves. Then came the Perioci who dwelt in the surrounding regions and had their own administration but owed allegiance to the Spartans and paid them tribute. Lastly there were the Helots who were slaves attached to the land which they cultivated for the benefit of the Equals.

As soon as they were five years old, the Spartan children were taken away from their mothers and submitted to a harsh military discipline and a communal life. When they became adolescents they had to undergo a severe initiation to manhood and continued to take one meal a day together. Then came also the test of blood when every young Spartan was constrained to kill a Helot. Indeed the young Spartan had to give himself up either to the profession of arms or to the service of the State, whereas the Helots, decendants of the original

Achaean population, enslaved and deprived of all civil rights, remained at the mercy of the conqueror.

This powerful aristocratic and military state was the prototype of all dictatorships and finished by dominating nearly the whole of the Peloponnesus until the time came when the brutal excesses of Spartan policy united all the rest of Greece against them. Finally the victory of Leuctra (371) liberated the Hellenes from this intolerable tyranny.

It was at this time that Epaminondas ravaged the countryside of Laconia and organized the isolation of Sparta by creating the fortified cities of Messenia, Megalopolis and Mantines.

Vainly did King Cleomenes II (235–219) attempt to reintroduce the laws of Lycurgus, for, after he was defeated in 221, Sparta lost her outlying provinces, and ended by being dominated by the Romans in 146 B.C. Captured and destroyed by Alaric the Goth in 396, what remained of Sparta was ravaged by Slav incursions in the 9th century and the population emigrated to the Mani in the extreme south of the peninsula.

Sparta was repopulated by the Byzantines but in 1248 the French abandoned it to install themselves at Mistra whilst they were building a string of fortresses in the Parnon and Taygetus. In 1296 Guillaume de Villehardouin handed over Mistra and part of his possessions to Michael Paleologus to pay for his ransom and so, for more than two centuries, the land was ruled by despots of that family until the arrival of the Turks.

There remains little of the ancient Sparta described by Pausanias. First of all, in Leonidas Street the so-called tomb of Leonidas is nothing else but a little Hellenistic temple with a *pronaos* and a *cella*. By retracing our steps, we shall find, near the modern stadium, a path which crosses an olive grove and leads to what was the southern gate of the Acropolis near to which are to be found the remains of a Roman colonnade. The back wall has no less than 25 *exedra* with niches. Ruins of two Byzantine churches lie inside the medieval *kastro*. The largest was a basilica with three aisles built in the 10th century and enlarged in the 11th. A chapel of the 11th century contains the tomb of S. Nico.

The theatre, which has been hollowed out of the slopes of the Acropolis, dates from the 2nd or 1st century B.C., and the tiers of white marble of its auditorium have been used for the construction of Mistra. Likewise the *nymphaeum* was built at a later date with materials from the theatre. The stage shows remains of masonry of various periods.

Among the different remains on the right bank of the Eurotes, we should note the ancient *Limnaion* or sanctuary of Artemis Orthis which is composed of a small temple and of a horseshoe-shaped Roman theatre which embraces half of the ancient temple. It was here that the ritual flogging of the young Spartans took place and they transformed it into a test of endurance.

Finally in the museum are to be found *stele*, carvings, bas-reliefs and bronze figurines, though two Roman mosaics have been left in the villas where they were originally laid.

ITINERARY VI

THE PELOPONNESUS II—MISTRA TO SICYON BY WAY OF OLYMPIA

Mistra — Monemvasia — Gythion — Areopolis — Kalamata — Koroni — Pylos — Methoni — Messena — Megalopolis — Karytaina — Bassae — Olympia — Gastouni — Andravida — Chlemoutsi — Kyllini — Patras — Megaspilaion — Sicyon.

WE should follow the road to Mistra which goes towards the Taygetus Range in which appear two deep gaps. The first—the Gap of Parori to the south—is dominated by the Rock of the Apothetes from which the Spartans threw their deformed babies.

We shall soon arrive in sight of the mountain, crowned by the imposing Frankish fortress, on the slopes of which the ruins of the Byzantine city are enclosed in the ancient ramparts together with churches and palaces which are still intact.

Mistra developed in all its splendour in 1349 when it became the residence of the sons or brothers of the Emperors of Byzantium who were given the task of governing the Morea. Thus, Manuel Cantacuzene and his brother Mathew were succeeded by several generations of Paleologues: Theodore I from 1383 to 1407, Theodore II, Constantine Dragatses and Demetrius. In 1460, Mistra reverted to the Turks; from 1687 to 1715 to the Venetians. In 1770, the town was burnt down by the Albanians at the time of the revolt of the Morea, and from that time on it was more or less abandoned.

At MISTRA there is a remarkable group of Byzantine churches which demonstrate the brilliance of the artistic and intellectual life which animated the Court of these despots. The famous philosopher Gemiste Plethon, who was born about 1360 and died in 1452, founded at Mistra a secret brotherhood. He professed a spiritualism inspired by Plato, which repudiated Christianity and preached the restoration of a refined paganism. This shows how deeply the Byzantine humanists who stayed at Mistra were sensitive to the seductive influence of pagan thought and notably to the neo-Platonism which had never ceased to have followers since the time of Psellos.

If we approach the town by the path which runs near the fountain of the Marmara we begin by veering to the left and leaving, to the right, the charming chapel of St. George which is partly restored. It is a private chapel like so many at Mistra. We then arrive at the Monastery of the Peribleptos dominated by a tower in the Italian manner and still surrounded by the exceptionally well-preserved walls dating from the 14th century and defended by a battlemented tower.

The Church of the Peribleptos contains the most beautiful series of frescoes in Mistra. They were carried out during the time of the first despot, Manuel Cantacuzene, son of the Emperor John VI and of his wife Isabelle de Lusignan. This is proved by the presence of the coats of arms of the two families, rampant lions and fleur-de-lis, figuring in the plaques embedded in the walls.

They bear witness to the evolution brought to Byzantine art by the mystical speculations of the hesychastes monks with whom the Cantacuzenes were in league, to ward off the dangers of social and intellectual revolution brought about by zealots and humanists. Hesychasm was a creed based on the possibility of man seeing God in the virtue of the mystery of the Incarnation and in the grace brought by the sacraments of baptism, confirmation and the Eucharist as well as attendance at the liturgies. This led to the greater decoration of the apses with icons because it was there that the liturgies were celebrated. Subjects which had formerly been used separately, were now used together, enriched with new themes of liturgical significance.

The Peribleptos is one of the most ancient buildings in which was established this Iconographic system which we find again developed in the churches and the monasteries, notably on Mount Athos. As well as the traditional image of the *Virgin Enthroned Between Two Angels* and *The Ascension*, in the *bema*, there used to be the *Lamb of God*, ancient symbol of the Sacrifice of Christ, John Chrysostomos, celebrating the liturgy in the Prosthesis with the assistance of an angel-deacon, *The Communion of the Apostles* and the prefiguration in the Old Testament of the Eucharistic sacrifice, Philoxenis and the Sacrifice of Abraham. The divine liturgy was depicted in the prosthesis and in the *diaconicon*, Christ Emmanuel appeared, sleeping with open eyes between two angels who were watching over him.

Particularly noteworthy is the *Divine Liturgy* in the prosthesis of the Peribleptos where angels, wrapped in great Dalmatian cloaks ridged with long luminous folds, take part in the procession of the Great Entry, whilst Christ, clothed as a Bishop, stands behind the altar, giving the blessing with His right hand and His left, touching the tabernacle where the closed Testament lies. Three angel-deacons on his right, wear on their heads the paten covered with an embroidered veil and are followed by three angel-priests who hold the chalices. The return of this procession is depicted to the left of Christ. An angel-deacon dispenses incense while others carry chandeliers. Above Christ, symbolizing the Trinity, the *Ancient of Days* is represented flanked by two seraphim who carry liturgical fans as well as the Dove of the Holy Ghost.

"This fresco," said Charles Delvoye, "evokes for the faithful the continuance of the Hymn of the Cherubim sung by the

Choirs during the Great Entry. It is, at the same time, an illustration of the secret prayer recited in a low voice, by the celebrant whilst this hymn is being chanted : 'It is thou who offerest and art offered, who receivest and art given, oh Christ our God.' From the point of view of technique, the contrast between the light, white draperies and the brown faces relieved by a few small touches of light add still more to the strange character and supernatural atmosphere of this scene which takes on the aspect of a mystical vision."

We must now stop to admire *The Ascension* in the *bema*, and *The Nativity* in the vaults of the south transept. It is extremely original and astonishingly modern in composition. We must note also in the west nave, *The Transfiguration* where Christ stands so nobly posed, in the dome; *Christ Pantocrator* in the south aisle, episodes from *The Childhood of the Virgin* as well as the astonishing *Sacrifice of Abraham* with all its purity and expressiveness of line.

The painters of the Peribleptos seem to be inspired by miniatures, because of their minute technique of exquisite touches, fine accurate lines and the employment of sumptuous colours in which deep tones predominate. They belong to the tradition of the aristocratic art of Constantinople, characterized by light, graceful figures and they enchant us by their poetic unreality and mysticism, entirely different from the realism of Italian art of the period. They affect us even more deeply because they are in sympathy with the most refined taste of our own time.

We must continue to follow the path which now goes up to the monastery of the Pantanassa which stands above the ruins of the House of Krevatas of the 18th century. To the left we see the façade of the Frangopoulos House of the 15th century, opposite the chapel of S. Kyriaki with, higher up, the ruins of the Church of Taxiarques.

We now arrive at the monastery of the Pantanassa (the Queen of the World), still occupied by a few nuns. The church, was built in 1420 in the reign of the Despot Theodore II Paleologue, by his prime minister John Phrangopoulos who also showed his gratitude to the Virgin for the miracles she had wrought. It has a splendid apse with a central alcove of 7 sections framed by 2 apsidioles with 6 sections pierced with 2 rows of windows whose arches rest on columns, the lower ones being in tierspoint, whilst between the two storeys, reversed arcades end in palmettes. The belfry, at the intersection of the north and west porticoes, is of French inspiration with its broken arches, its *oculi* with trifoliate openings and corner turrets. The basilica is on a cruciform plan with 5 domes for the upper galleries.

The frescoes, executed in about 1420, on the arches and in the galleries, are the work of local artists and their iconography is in part borrowed from the Peribleptos. This is also shown by the many-coloured cloak of one of the Hierosolymitans of the *Entry into Jerusalem*. The technique and the detail of the design is very much in the manner of the artists of the Peribleptos, but with far more nervous action in the attitudes of the characters and a tenderness in their expressions. We should note also the use of architectural backgrounds and of high rocks with deep fissures.

There is vitality and superb draughtsmanship in the realistic portrayal of *The Resurrection*, *The Raising of Lazarus*, *The Annunciation*, *The Presentation*, *The Strewing of the Palms*, *The Transfiguration*, the portrait of Manuel Chatzikis, in the narthex, and the *Hymn of Acathistes* in the aisles.

We leave the monastery by the opposite way and arrive at the Gate of Monemvasia in a tower through which we penetrate into the upper town. We continue along the foot of a tall house of the 15th century with battlements and arcades. Then, leaving on the left the pathway to the Church of St. Nicholas and the Small Palace, we can see to the right a mosque and then we shall arrive at the Palace of the Despot which stands upon a terrace dominating the district of the Brontochion.

We first of all see a rectangular building, more ancient, which doubtless dates from the first Stratagus, then the kitchens with their reservoirs of water in the basement. The austere façades have occasional lanceolate windows. The first despots of the family of the Cantacuzene united these two parts of the building and raised up upon their continuation to the west a structure with two storeys proceeded to the north by a portico and including a chapel with a central hall on the first floor.

Later, from about 1383, the Paleologues raised up on the right hand corner a great building of three storeys with the throne room extending above a portico with two storeys. Its façade has windows with trilobed arches in the flamboyant Italian style and, in the middle, the alcove for the throne extends with corbels surmounted by the arms of the Paleologues. Small circular windows open at the top of the façade.

In order to climb even higher, we must leave to the left a Turkish bath and reach the Church of St. Sophia built in 1350 by Manuel Comnenus. Here we can see the remains of the iconostasis and of the floor as well as several paintings including *Christ in Majesty* in the conch of the apse and *The Ascension* in the arch of the sanctuary. Besides the remains of the refectory and the monastic cells, the little chapel, which projects from over the north portico, contains a group of paintings including, on the cupola, *Christ Surrounded by Celestial Power* and, on the walls, *The Annunciation*, *The Passion of Christ*, *The Dormition of the Virgin* and *The Resurrection.*

In the chapel some other frescoes have been found beneath the whitewash: the figure of Christ, *The Virgin at Prayer* and the *Nativity of the Virgin.*

We then pass under a little aqueduct which supplied water to the upper town and climb up to the castle built by Guillaume de Villehardouin, the great nephew of the chronicler. It was restored by the Turks.

The gate of the castle is cut into the redan of the outer *enceinte* and protected by a high tower constructed, like the gate, by the Byzantines. This outer *enceinte* terminates, to the south, with a rectangular platform erected above a cistern and a circular bastion. A ramp gives access to the gate through which we enter into the keep protected by a great badly ruined tower erected by the Franks above a cistern. Inside the keep are the ruins of two little chapels which the Turks converted into a mosque.

We now go down as far as the Church of St. Sophia and take to the right a little lane flanked by a very beautiful Byzantine house called the *Little Palace* where a stairway enables us to reach the church of St. Nicholas which dates from the 18th century and whose paintings are banal. We go back to the Monemvasia Gate and descend to the church of the Evenghelistria which dates from the 14th century and still retains its frescoes of that period.

Almost immediately we come upon the Church of SS. Theodores, built before 1296 and one of the last churches with simulated corners of an architectural style originating in Constantinople but submitted to the influence of local tradition in Greece. The groined arches and the galleries have been replaced by barrel vaults and the exterior with rows of carefully dressed bricks is extremely elegant. The absence of niches on the façade accentuates the Greek character of the architecture.

The paintings of the interior are very badly faded. We can just make out the *Angel of the Annunciation* to the left of the entry to the sanctuary and, in the chapel to the left, the *Emperor Manuel Paleologue kneeling in front of the Theotokos* and, in the one on the right, scenes from the *Life of the Virgin*.

This church used to be part of the Monastery of Bronthocion, like *Hodighitria* which we shall see a little later. It was built in about 1312, on the plan of a basilica with three aisles and galleries where barrel vaults take the thrust of the dome.

It is the traditional form of the churches in the plan of the inscribed Greek cross. The prototype is the Church of St. Irene in Constantinople built six hundred years earlier. As in so many of the churches in Constantinople, the central dome is surrounded by four corner cupolas and by a sixth on the narthex. Between the arms of the cross, the upper corners have calottes instead of barrel vaults. The plan of the central apse with seven facets as well as its exterior aspect with decoration of arcades of brick, is inspired by the architecture of Constantinople. It is from Constantinople also that the idea of encircling the building with porticoes on three sides came and, as in the great monuments of the capital, the lower part of the walls of the interior were faced with marble which has now disappeared.

Finally the fresco workers who decorated the church came from Constantinople. They made use of a restrained number of colours, being particularly fond of deep blues, greens, browns, soft pink and cerise red, using them in the most harmonious combinations. They had a sensitive touch and their characters with elegant outlines are enveloped in mystery as is particularly apparent in the *Martyrs* of the west wall of the north chapel with heads with a spiritual expression full of gentleness, painted in delicate velvety colours.

We should notice particularly the *Miracles of Christ*, in the chapel at the extreme north of the narthex the portrait of Theodore I Paleologue as a despot and as a monk, as well as a group of saints at the southern extremity of the hall. On the south side of the church in a chapel where there are several tombs, a beautiful *Assumption of the Virgin* has been recently discovered. Several frescoes have also been brought to light in the central aisle.

We now come back as far as the last important church of Mistra, the *Metropolis*, or *St. Demetrios*, built between about 1291–1309 by the Metropolitan Nicephoros Moschopoulos. Originally it had a basilican plan, but in imitation of the

25. MISTRA : METROPOLIS.

26. MISTRA: CHURCH OF SS. THEODORES.

church of Hodighitria, a storey was added as in domed churches and this caused the painting of the main nave to be damaged. A number of marble carvings of the 9th and 11th centuries were reused in the decoration, notably in the north doorway and in the iconostasis. The parapet of the galleries dates from the 15th century.

The early artists who decorated this cathedral have none of the elegance and mastery of technique of the men whose work we have seen in earlier buildings. The characters are posed less realistically and they stand out of the scenes represented with an expression of calm simplicity. These paintings decorate the *prosthesis*, the base of the *diaconicon* and the left aisles where we can see the *Adolescence of the Virgin* and *The Miracles of Christ in Galilee.* In each episode the number of figures is limited and the background of architecture and rocks is treated diagrammatically.

The school of painters who some years later undertook the decoration of the central nave, the top of the *diaconicon* and the narthex, showed much more boldness and mastery of technique. The figures are more numerous and the composition is more skilfully conceived. The design of the architectural backgrounds shows more imagination, the gestures of the figures are more expressive and the draughtsmanship much more sensitive. The harmony of the colours is more vibrant and the contrast deeper. Unfortunately these works are in a bad state of preservation. The figures of angels in the *Last Judgement* in the narthex are specially to be admired.

A third school, which carried out the decorations in the south aisle, had something in common with the earlier one and these paintings delight us with their graceful design and sense of movement, notably in *The Entombment of St. Demetrios*, the *Man with Dropsy* and *The Leper.*

On the left side of the church, there is a pretty courtyard with two rows of balconies and a museum where decorative fragments found in the ruins are displayed. Of particular interest is a bas-relief of the beginning of the 15th century, *Christ Enthroned*. Treated as a flat surface with deep incisions and no modelling, it is a kind of engraving on stone rather than an example of sculpture.

We can leave by the well-preserved Gate of Marmara through a vaulted passage.

A little further on, beyond the town walls, the Church of St. John has some 15-century paintings, more particularly a *Crucifixion*, whilst the little Church of St. Christopher which we pass before leaving is covered with 15th-century frescoes.

It is a forty-five minutes' walk to reach the foot of the Castle which is perched high upon a detached spur of the Parnon Range. After passing a chapel which has been restored but still has a few frescoes, we come to the 12th-century church of Haghia Paraskevi, and then to yet another chapel with frescoes.

The southern front of the rampart is in a fair state of preservation with a strip of curtain wall linking two towers. Below the entrance, a church with a single aisle has a few frescoes.

Inside the *enceinte*, Haghios Georgios is the best preserved of all the churches of Geraki. Though it dates back to the 13th century, it still has some frescoes, and an iconastasis with an ikon of St. George.

To the east, the wall of the fortress has a strip of rampart with a staircase leading up to the battlement walk. A cistern carved out of the rock can still be seen and, to the south of the castle on the extension of the rocky spur, three other churches, of which the last is decorated with frescoes; one of these depicting Joshua attacking a city of the Amalakites, dates from the first half of the 14th century.

If the Geraki road is still bad, we can take the asphalt road to Gythion, leaving it at the 24th kilometre for a road to the left which goes to Monemvasia via Skala. It is asphalted for the greater part of the way. We pass, first of all, through some marshes, and then climb up to a highly picturesque mountain region. After having driven half-way up the slope of a mountain, we shall catch sight of the rocky islet on which is situated the curious little town of MONEMVASIA connected to the mainland by a narrow isthmus. Before reaching this place, we shall find, at the water's edge, an hotel with a terrace where fish and even lobster are served.

This promontory, three hundred metres high, which the Byzantines had transformed into an islet, linked to the mainland by a causeway crossing over a fortified bridge, was called *Minos* by the Ancients. When the Slav invasions began, it served as a place of refuge for the Greeks of Laconia, and it became, under the name Monemvasia, a fortress and at the same time a very prosperous commercial port. In 1147, this city repelled an attack by the Normans of Sicily, but in 1249 it was besieged by Guillaume de Villehardouin, and captured after three years when the inhabitants were forced through starvation to surrender. In order to pay for a ransom he was compelled to hand it over to the Emperor of Byzantium in 1263. It was then held in turn by the Papacy, the Venetians and the Turks who repulsed an attack by la Valette, the Grand Master of Malta, in 1654. In 1821, the insurgent Greeks took over Monemvasia when it was renamed Malvoisie after the celebrated wine which was very popular in the late Middle Ages. The vines have entirely disappeared in this region but the plants sent to Santorin, Cyprus, Sicily, Sardinia and Portugal still produce vintages that are much appreciated.

The town occupies the southern slope of the promontory and is protected by a wall that goes right down to the water's edge. It is cut by a gateway surmounted by a coat of arms and leading into a long, winding passage. Another gate, higher up the hill, provides access to the Upper Town. The old Byzantine rampart was rebuilt by the Turks in the 16th century.

The Lower Town is charming with its fortified houses and its churches lining the main street or scattered in the narrow lanes that are broken in places by stairways and vaulted archways. The little hotels here are very unpretentious but very clean, and it certainly would be tempting to spend a few days in one of them to enjoy the peace and nostalgic atmosphere of the past. There is no electricity on the island and the streets are lit with big petrol lamps fixed to the walls. Incidentally cars are not allowed within the city walls.

The churches of the Lower Town are not very old: *Haghios Nicolaos* only dates back to 1703; *Our Lady of Crete* from the beginning of the 18th century, *Haghios Stephanos* of *Crete* from the 16th century. This last church is Italo-Byzantine in style and contains an ikon of Christ Elkomemos, that is to say, of Christ being dragged up on to the Cross. *Haghia Anna* is a 14th-century basilica, restored in 1697 by the Venetians.

From the Upper Town, a path leads to the Citadel which occupies the top of the promontory dominating the whole city. The northern side of the Citadel was defended by a curtain wall flanked by two towers. It was erected by the Venetians in the 16th century and restored later on by the Turks.

Inside the Citadel we can see the remains of a little fort of the Byzantine era as well as the *Church of Haghia Sophia* which was founded by Adronicus (1287–1328). This is the most interesting ecclesiastical building on the island and is constructed on the same plan as the basilica of Daphni; it contains frescoes of martyred saints.

After retracing our steps along the road by which we came, we must continue our way to Gythion, a good centre from which to visit the peninsula of Mani.

GYTHION is a pleasant and peaceful little port with lines of white houses along the quayside where there are two or three unpretentious hotels. Founded originally by the Minyens, and then a port of call of the Phoenicians, it became the arsenal and principal harbour of Sparta. The town is dominated by Mount Moumaro, which was the ancient *Larysion*. Just beyond the pier, the Island of Marathonisi was *Kranae*, and it is now connected with the mainland by a causeway. It was here that stood Migonium, a suburb of the old city which was open to traders and merchants from the East.

For a while, Kranae was a Phoenician centre for the sale of purple dye. It was also noted as a place of asylum, and so it was that Paris took refuge here after his seduction of Helen. In Migonium a sanctuary of Aphrodite was founded by the Phoenicians and may have stood on the site of the Metropolitan Church of Haghios Gorgios.

The island is deserted in the present day, though it has a lighthouse and its shores are lined with trees and shrubs. In the centre, a small ruined Kastro has been restored by the town council, so that it is now a charming feature of the landscape.

The crest of the Larysion, formerly dedicated to Dionysus, is crowned by the ruins of another Kastro. At the base of the mountain, to the left of the road by which we came, a cubic altar carved out of the rock is said to be the Sanctuary of Zeus Terastios, a fact which is confirmed by an inscription on the face of the cliff. It is identified with the Altar of Zeus Kappotas where Orestes sat and was cured of his madness.

The old town was 250 metres to the north, beyond the stream named Selenitsa. To the left, the triangular hill of the Acropolis still has some fragments of the original wall. The remains of a theatre hollowed out of the base of the hill are in a better state of preservation. Next to it have been discovered the foundations of a building which must have been the Temple of Augustus and Tiberius who were worshipped according to important laws regulating the worship of Emperors.

As the level of the coast has sunk since the days of Antiquity, other ruins are submerged, but they can be seen from the quayside and from the beach.

We should now take the road leading to Areopolis and across this peninsula of the Mani which is interesting not only because of the beauty of the landscape, but also because of the character of the inhabitants, their habits, their traditions and the architecture of their fortified houses.

The Mani, or Maniots, descended from the Laconians who had fled from the Slav invasions of the Taygetus, have always displayed great courage and a high degree of independence towards the successive masters of the Morea: Byzantines, Franks, Venetians or Turks. They lived in clans which had at their head archons or beys who treated with the occupying force on terms of equality. They lived in fortified houses which are like castle keeps with battlements and machicolation. If the Turks invaded their countryside, they abandoned their dwelling and sought refuge in the hills with their wives and children and waged guerrilla warfare on their enemies.

The history of the Mani abounds in deeds of arms of great heroism.

In the 16th century, the Genoese transported a number of them to south-western Corsica.

The road, asphalted to start with, is bad for the greater part of the next trip, more especially between Areopolis and Kalamata.

At the 8th kilometre we shall find, at the face of a wooded mountain, the Frankish Castle of PASSAVA, built by the Marshal of Morea, Jean de Neuilly, and restored by the Turks in the 17th century.

We next come to the arid and rocky Land of the Mani, with its bare mountains divided up by valleys where grow olive trees and a few cypresses to break the monotony of the landscape. After having crossed the whole of the Peninsula, we come near to the western shore with a fine panorama of the Bay and the village of Itylo at the foot of the Taygetus Range, and on the right the Fort of Kelepha built by the Turks in the first half of the 17th century and captured by Morosini in 1685.

We now come to AREOPOLIS, the most important township of the Mani. It is attractive because of its white houses surrounding the Church of Ayios Taxiarkhis, built in 1798 by the Mavromichalis. It looks far older because of its Italianate bas-relief executed in the Renaissance manner.

From here we can proceed to the grottoes of VLYCHADA, discovered a few years ago and which have recently been adapted for visits.

First of all we take the road to Pyrgos, and on reaching this place, take the road to the right which leads to the coast and the entrance to the grotto.

This grotto with its numerous stalactites and stalagmites which often join together to form a single column, is nothing else than an underground river which can be explored by boat in a trip taking half an hour. It is among the most attractive caves in the whole of Europe.

The villages in the region of Pyrgos are most unusual and interesting because of their fortified houses and little Byzantine churches. One kilometre away from the town there is the village of Haghias Marina with its 12th-century church, and a little further on the church of Haghios Petros which appears to belong to the same period. Then there is the village of Karouda which has an 11th-century church but with frescoes of a later date, whilst Dryalos is dominated by high towers. A 14th-century building adjoins a more recently constructed church, but on the same slope of the mountain there is Vamkava where the church of Haghias Theodoros was built in 1075.

All these places are to be found within a radius of a few kilometres. Towards Kitta there is, a little further on to the right by the roadside, the small monastery of Phaneromeni, dating from the end of the 11th century, but restored since then. Then on the left, the church of Haghios Sotir was built in the 12th or 13th centuries and, before arriving at Kitta, the church of St. Sergius and St. Bacchus, better known as

Haghios Georgios, was founded at the end of the 11th century but has been restored. Incidentally the village of Kitta has even more character than its neighbours. However, we should also note Bourlarioi where the church of Haghios Strategos has a carved marble ikon.

The road terminates at YEROLIMIN, a small fishing hamlet situated at the end of a creek, dominated by a high cliff.

Three kilometres away, the ruins of three paleo-Christian basilicas have been discovered at Alika, the *Kainopolis* of Classical times.

By caïque, or in two hours on foot, it is possible to get to Cape Matapan, ancient *Taenaron*, where there was a Temple of Poseidon. It was the centre of the Confederation of the Eleuthero-Laconians at the same time as the shrine of an oracle, but on occasion it also served as a place of refuge from pirates. Some vestiges of this building are to be found in the wall of the chapel on Assomaton, near to the Bay of the Kisternae, where was the former port of Psamathos.

To the west was the cave from which Hercules dragged Cerberus out of Hell, and to the north of the Bay of Porto Cayxo can be discerned, on the heights, the insignificant remains of the Frankish fortress of Mani, called *"La Grande Kaigne"* in the medieval French chronicles. It was built in 1250 by Guillaume de Villehardouin but surrendered to the Byzantines in 1263.

It may well be quite a problem to get luncheon, as few tourists find their way to this region. It is probably best to go on to Limenion, the port of Areopolis, a very picturesque village with fortified houses, churches and cypresses set out in tiers on the slopes of a mountain. There is a taverna here specializing in fish but it is not always open. If it is not open, the only thing to do is to go on to ITYLO, reached by a road winding up to the top of the hill on which it stands. Just below it, stands the church of the 18th-century convent of

27. MONEMVASIE : ST. SOPHIE.

28. KORONI.

29. METHONI: BOURZI TOWER.

30. THEATRE OF MEGALOPOLIS.

Dekoulos, and in the main square, the church of Haghios Sotir which contains a beautiful ikon of carved gilded wood. Itylo is the ancient *OETYLOS*, a town of the Eleuthero-Laconian Confederation.

If it is impossible to get a proper meal in this place, the owner of the café may agree to prepare eggs and bread or salad bought from a nearby shop.

Ten kilometres further on, the road passes near to a stalagmite grotto at Dirou.

Next we come to two villages with a number of ancient churches and chapels for the most part of the 13th century. At KOUTIPHARI, the ancient *Thalamea*, there are the churches of Haghia Sophia and of the Metamorphosis. At PLATSA, there are the churches of Haghios Nicolaos, Haghia Paraskevi and Haghios Demetrios. We shall see three more charming churches to the right of the road, and a little further on, one to the left which was attached to an ancient nunnery with some modest buildings disposed round a courtyard.

Next, we come to Kardamyli which has an 18th-century and Venetian fortress.

Beyond this point the road is asphalted once more and passes through KAMBOS, dominated by the Fortress of Zarnata built on the site of the former village of *Alagonia* which is mentioned by Pausanias. The medieval curtain wall embodies vestiges of a wall of polygonal masonry of the Hellenic Age. The Tower was built in the 18th century. After having belonged to the Paleologues of Mistra, the Castle was occupied by the Turks but surrendered without a struggle in 1685 to the Venetian Morosini.

The road descends towards the sea and the very fertile Plain of Messena and finally reaches KALAMATA, a prosperous little town where the Hotel Rex is really comfortable. It is possible also to stay at the motel on the beach which has to be passed on the way to the town.

Kalamata, the capital of the *nome* (province) of Messena,

has a very busy harbour from which the different products of the southern Peloponnesus are exported. It was the *Pherae* of Homer which doubtless belonged to Menelaus, for it appears on the list of the seven cities which Agamemnon promised to Achilles in order to appease his anger. When Telemachus was going from Pylos to Sparta and stopped at Pherae, it was not by the seashore, but at the foot of the Taygetus and on the site of the present village of Kalami.

In 1206 the region was conquered from the Byzantines by Guillaume de Champlitte, first Prince of Morea, and by his lieutenant, Geoffroy de Villehardouin, whom he appointed Lord of Kalamata. Guillaume II de Villehardouin was born at Kalamata in 1218 and died there in 1278. Annexed to the states of the despots of Mistra towards 1425, it was captured by the Turks and held by them until it was taken by the Venetians in 1685 in whose hands it remained until the recapture by the Turks in 1715.

The *Kastro* or Castle of the Villehardouins was built by the Franks in 1208 on the site of the ancient Acropolis of Pherae. The Byzantines strengthened the fortress and built a monastery within its walls. The keep was constructed in the 13th century on the site of a previous Byzantine church. Remodelled in 1293, it was badly damaged by the Turks who blew it up in 1685 together with the north-eastern bastion which was restored by the Venetians. The main gateway of the fortress is surmounted by the Lion of St. Mark.

Within the confines of the city, and in the Bazaar, the 10th-century Byzantine Church of St. Anne serves as a choir to a larger church of Italian style built in 1626. The belfry is of Italo-Norman design.

From Kalamata we will go to Pylos to visit the fortresses of Koroni and Methoni, but as there is no proper road between these two castles, we shall have to turn back from Methoni and return by Pylos in order to go to Methoni.

Most of the road to Koroni has been asphalted, and it hugs

the coast for the greater part of the way. The countryside is prosperous and the hills are covered with olive groves.

The whitewashed houses of KORONI extend along the promontory between its small harbour and its imposing Turkish and Venetian fortress.

It is the site of the ancient *Asine*. In the Middle Ages, the inhabitants of *Koroni*, which lay further to the north, established themselves there and gave it the name of the city which they had just left. Guillaume de Champlitte and Geoffroy de Villehardouin captured it in 1205 but were driven out of it a year later by the Venetians. The town was plundered by the Turks in 1428 but, in 1500, the inhabitants rose against the Venetians and handed over the city to the Turks. In 1622, it fell into the hands of the Spanish, but was taken over once more by the Venetians and later by the Turks.

The Byzantine fortress occupied the western point of the promontory but the Venetians enclosed the whole of the summit within a wall and, in the 16th century, the Turks added to the eastern side a powerful building with batteries for artillery.

The castle is entered by a Gothic gateway on the north front which faces the sea. This rampart was modified later on for the installation of a battery. To the right of this gateway, we shall notice massive blocks of stone taken from the site of *Asine*.

After having passed through the gate and turned to the left, we come upon a structure composed of two circular bastions, one of which is surrounded by an enormous embankment. Further on, at the foot of the ramparts, a platform is protected by an enormous outwork and a ditch in front of which is a counterscarp. A strong casemate rises up at each extremity of the platform, one of which was destroyed in 1944. All this part of the fortress was built by the Turks in the 16th century.

On the eastern side, the edge of the cliff serves as a natural rampart; it is reinforced by a bastion, and an inscription states that this part was repaired by the Venetians to fill up a breach made during the siege of 1685 by Morosini.

By continuing to walk round the citadel, we shall come upon the wall of the ancient Byzantine fort which was included within the fortified perimeter when it was enlarged by the Venetians. The western point is marked by a bastion raised by the Venetians in 1463.

In the interior of the fortress there are gardens, private houses and the remains of an important basilica. Only the left hand apse is still standing and has served as a chapel. Close by are the domes of the church of a Byzantine monastery.

After our inspection of the castle we must retrace our way to the fork of the Pylos road. It passes through a hilly region covered with oak trees between Maglada and Lykodimo before it reaches the Bay of Navarino. There is a magnificent panorama of this splendid anchorage protected by the island of Sphacteria and stretching between the straits of Sykia and the Straits of Megalo-Thouro.

PYLOS is a pleasant little town built by the French. The Venetians called it Navarino, derived from Avarino, the Castle of the Avars, the name which the Byzantines had given to the Acropolis of Pylos after the Slav invasions.

In 1573 the Turks built a citadel with six bastions and battlemented walls at the foot of Mount Haghios Nicolaos. It was called Neo Kastro to distinguish it from the Old Castle of Pylos. The Venetians captured it in 1686 and kept it until 1715.

In 1825, Ibrahim Pasha made it the base of his operations in Messena which were executed with such savagery that they provoked the intervention of the European powers which brought about the liberation of Greece by the Battle of Navarino. Great Britain, France and Russia had decided to enter into official relations with the insurgents, and to impose an armistice which the Turks refused to accept. So it was that allied squadrons, commanded by Admirals Codrington, de Rigny and Heiden, sailed into the Bay of Navarino with 27 warships and 1,276 cannon on the 20th of October 1827. In the roadstead was anchored a Turco-Egyptian fleet of 89 warships with 2,438 cannon and 10,000 men. The allies intended to intimidate Ibrahim Pasha and force him to stop ravaging the population of Messena, without however resorting to fighting, but some random shots fired by the Turks provoked an open conflict. By nightfall the Turkish fleet was reduced to 29 small vessels and had lost 6,000 men. The Allied fleet had had some casualties but had not lost a single ship. The King of England qualified this victory as a deplorable misunderstanding, but at any rate it was a misunderstanding that hastened the liberation of Greece.

A number of different monuments have been erected to heroes and victims of this battle on the Island of Sphacteria. It is on this island that 420 Spartans were surrounded by the Athenians in a fort with square towers, of which the remains can still be seen on a plateau. After a desperate resistance, the Spartans had to surrender to the Athenians who were led by Demosthenes and Cleon.

The small town of Pylos is pleasant enough but of no archaeological interest, though we can visit the fortress of Avarino, or Paleokastro, whose battlemented walls and round towers are built in places on the foundations of the ancient Acropolis reconstructed by Epaminondas. There is an outer *enceinte* and a redoubt surrounding a rectangular courtyard. At the foot of the cliff, a cave known as Nestor's Grotto communicated by an upper exit with the *kastro*. This cave is full of stalactites in the shape of animals which may be the source of the legend that Nestor wished to keep his herds here. There is also the cave where Hermes hid the oxen which he had stolen from Apollo and where he hung up the skins of the animals that he had slaughtered.

One can also see, on the summit of a hill on the way to

Methoni, the Turkish castle with a vast battlemented ring of ramparts with an ancient mosque in the centre.

The little town of METHONI is situated on a promontory with the extremity occupied by the well-preserved remains of a Byzantine fortress which was enlarged by the Venetians. It would be as famous as the ramparts of Rhodes if the walls were better kept and repaired.

Methoni, or *Mothone*, was a Messenian city given by the Spartans to the Nauplians who remained in occupation there until Messena was set free by Epaminondas. In 431 the Athenians besieged the city without success. In A.D. 533, the Byzantine General Belisarius put in at Methoni on his way to North Africa to launch a campaign against the Vandals. In 1125, Doge Domenico Michieli ordered the city to be razed to the ground. A Venetian fleet captured Methoni in 1206 and then fortified it. In 1500, Bajazet II besieged the garrison of 7,000 men with a force of 100,000 soldiers and 55 cannon, and forced the defenders to capitulate. Vainly the Knights of St. John of Rhodes in 1531, and then Don Juan of Austria, tried to recapture the city, though Morosini was successful in 1686 and the Venetians remained in possession until 1715. Finally, in 1828, the Turks had to surrender the place to General Maison.

A large ditch separates the fortress from the town by describing a semicircle at the base of the promontory. The counterscarp was composed of a walk protected by a glacis which has disappeared. It belongs to several different régimes, for the Venetians changed the plan at the beginning of the 18th century in order to take in a large bastion built by General Antonio Loredan. Opposite the bastion, on the counterscarp, is a stone shield with the Lion of St. Mark. All along the part of the counterscarp between the bastion and the bridge, there was, at that time, an underground passage connected with several different perpendicular galleries passing under the glacis so as to facilitate the digging of countermines.

The greater part of the ditch dates from the 15th century, as well as the outworks, the central part of the counterscarp and the glacis. The northern rampart, flanked with square towers which we see first of all, is set between two bastions, the Bembo Bastion of the 15th century to the west, and the Loredan Bastion of 1714 to the east. This last was adapted to be equipped with artillery. The bridge by which the ditch is crossed was built in 1828 to replace a wooden bridge. The door cut by the Venetians at the beginning of the 18th century, replaces an older gateway which was set further to the east.

After having passed through the first gateway, we must veer to the left, and then pass through a second gate, and then through a third called Porta di Terra Firma with immense arches in tierpoint dating from the first Venetian constructions, before coming into the interior of the fortress, opposite an antique column with a Byzantine capital.

Next we must skirt the rampart on the left, which is fortified with towers and with embrasures for rifle and artillery fire, built by the Turks on the arcades. One of these towers with a postern is adorned with a Lion of St. Mark set above two coats of arms of the Foscarini over a plaque with the crest of the Michieli.

The Turkish battery comes to an end at a big square tower in a ruinous condition which dates back perhaps to the Roman era or to the beginning of the Byzantine occupation. The eastern rampart which runs along the shore has a door providing an outlet on to a little wharf constructed in 1870.

At the southern extremity of the promontory there stands a high tower built by the Turks. Then, opposite the Sea Gate flanked by two towers reconstructed by the Turks with stones from the ruins, rises up the Bourzi Tower, a big round tower built by the Turks in the 16th century. The bridge which connected it to this entrance has disappeared.

The western rampart on a cliff is reinforced by six towers and it is among the first fortifications erected by the Venetians.

It comes to an end at a transversal wall which extends to the Porta di Terra Firma by which we entered the fortress and which stands next to a kind of outwork. In the centre of this wall a gateway leads through the central tower which abuts this rampart with four other towers built by the Turks in the 16th century.

Among the ruins in the interior of the part of the fortress which we have just visited are those of a Turkish Bath, of cisterns, of a powder magazine and of a minaret which was built on the site of what had been the Latin cathedral of Methone.

We can next visit the enormous Bambo bastion which was built in 1480, but remodelled later on by the Turks. It dominates another older bastion that can be reached by taking the passage on the right after the first door in the northern rampart. The battery on the western side was laid out by the Venetians in the 18th century, if we can judge by a Lion of St. Mark carved on the wall.

The western wall of the castle on the landward side was built at the end of the 15th century. It is adorned with a plaque with a winged lion and the coats of arms of the Bembo, the Foscarini and the Foscolo.

As we have already stated, this remarkable complex of fortifications ought to be better cared for and publicized.

On returning to Pylos and skirting a lagoon we continue on our way to Korythasion, a little village which can be seen on the left of the road. About ten minutes' walk to the south of the highway, a domed tomb has been discovered and another one of this type is also on the left of the road 4 kilometres further on. It is the royal tomb of *KATO ENGLIANO* of the Mycenaean era and is entered by a corridor carved out of the rock. Originally the gateway was surmounted by three lintels, of which only the middle one subsists, and the vault of the *tholos* has collapsed. On this site have been discovered the bones of human beings and of animals offered up for sacrifice : bulls, goats and sheep.

31. TEMPLE OF BASSAE.

32. OLYMPIA : HERAION.

A little further on, still on the left, is the *PALACE OF NESTOR* of the Mycenaean era; this Nestor who brought sixty vessels into the expedition against Troy. This must be the real palace of Pylos, the town founded by Neleus or his cousin Aphareus.

According to tradition, the south-west of the Peloponnesus was governed by the Nereids, a family which came from Iolkos near to the Volos of the present day. Nestor, who succeeded Neleus, turned Pylos into one of the richest cities of the Mycenaean age. After the capture of Troy, Nestor returned to Pylos and his descendants governed the land for two generations until the Doric invasion.

The remains of the palace, protected by a shed, are composed first of all of a *propylon* with an axial column with, on the left, two rooms reserved for the archives, whilst the guard room was on the right.

Next we penetrate into a courtyard facing a *megaron* with a two-columned portico between two *antae* and on the right a platform on which the sentry box must have stood. Then we come to a hall, whose walls were decorated with frescoes, with another sentry box, whilst a door led into the great hall of the *megaron* which had a roof resting on four wooden columns set up on stone bases. The plaster of the wall was adorned with frescoes. As at Mycenae and at Tiryns there was a great circular hearth between the four columns. The throne must have been on the right near two cupolas linked together by a little groove which may have been used for the royal libations.

Returning to the court which was faced by other rooms, the most important one on the left was preceded by a portico with two columns leading to a long corridor, whilst on the right there was a staircase to the next floor or to the terrace on the roof.

The queen's apartment was at the north-eastern corner with a Great Hall with a circular hearth, a sitting-room and a dressing-room, whilst the passage we have already mentioned led to waiting-rooms opposite a bathroom with a bath and, further on, a stairway led to the first floor. Finally in a whole series of warehouses, huge jars have been found as well as the remains of more than 3,000 cups.

Further on, the ruins of a still older palace were found and it was composed of two great rooms of which one opened out on to a portico with two fluted pillars. The walls were covered with painted stucco and there is a fresco of a battle scene where the defeated were being thrown down from the top of the ramparts of a captured citadel. The neighbouring room was perhaps the throne room and there must have been several dependencies.

To the left of the great palace, we can still see the remains of the foundations of a house and, to the north, a vast cellar preceded by a wall in which have been discovered numerous jars set up in holes in the ground. Further to the west, a huge building preceded by a ramp was perhaps the barracks of the guards or an administrative office. It comprised a courtyard with an altar situated in front of a small sanctuary.

Finally the lower town extended at the foot of the palace and all around a number of domed tombs have been excavated.

The visit of the Palace of Nestor must be completed by an inspection of the exhibits in the museum which include splendid Mycenaean vases, astonishing gold jewellery and fragments of frescoes of a beauty comparable to those which have been found in Crete.

This museum is not near the palace but in the neighbouring little town of CHORA.

People who are particularly interested in Byzantine art should go on to Filiatra, where a road on the left leads to CHRISTIANOU, to visit the metropolitan church of the former village of *Christianoupolis*, built in the third quarter of the 11th century.

This church is dedicated to the Transfiguration of Knowledge and has some carved fragments of the iconostasis. Christianoupolis was originally the seat of a bishopric but was transformed into an archbishopric towards the end of the 11th century when the present church was built.

After the conquest of the Peloponnesus by the Franks, the see was left vacant until their departure in 1283. Towards the end of the 14th century, the archbishopric became a suffragan of Corinth, though it survived the Turkish domination and was transferred to Kyparissia in 1837.

Also near to FILIATRA, at the place called Haghia Kuriaki, are to be found the remains of a five-aisled basilica, of the end of the 5th century or of the beginning of the 6th. The central nave was rebuilt before the end of the 6th century as it had been destroyed by an earthquake. Later a small chapel was erected on the ruins.

Returning to Kalamata by the Pylos road, we can set off from this place for Megalopolis, either by the direct road which is asphalted, or by making a detour to visit the ruins of Messena.

In this case there is no need to spend the night at Kalamata, for at Messena we can take the road to Labena which is asphalted. From the Kalamata Megalopolis road it is possible to go to Labena by taking, on the left, a road which passes through Meligala.

The road from Messena to Labena continues for 3 kilometres before arriving at Labena, at Eva Neo Chori, where a road to the left will lead us to the village of ANDROUSSA, 6 kilometres away. It is the *Druges* of the Chronicle of Morea which was, with Corinth, the seat of a military administration of French Morea. There we can see the ruins of a Frankish castle and, to the north, an ancient church dedicated to St. George.

Five kilometres from here, in a lonely valley at Samarina, the attractive church of the Zadochos Pighi erected in the reign of Adronicos Paleologus has kept some traces of its frescoes.

To the right, in the village of Labena, a road which climbs

up to a height, passes through Simisa and ends at the little village of Mavromati which occupies more or less the site of the ancient town of *MESSENA*, capital of Messenia, founded by Epaminondas after his victory of Leuctres over the Spartans in 371 B.C.

The fortifications of Messena are a splendid example of the skilful military constructions of the 4th century B.C. It turned the town into a huge entrenched camp on the site of the Ithome. Mavrimarti (the black eye) owes its name to the gushing spring, called also Calliehoi (ancient Clepsydra), which flows from an aqueduct across an old wall overgrown with bushes in the middle of the village.

With Megalopolis, Mantinea and Argos, Messena formed a group of strategic fortresses to contain Sparta. Messena was besieged in 214 B.C. by a general of Philip V, Demetrios of Pharos, who died in the course of the assault, then in 202 it was beleaguered by Nabis whom the Achaian Philopoemen forced to retreat. But the demagogue Dinocrates having incited the population to rebel against the Achaians, Philopoemen had to come and besiege the town and was made prisoner.

He was condemned to die by hemlock in 183, but his successor Lycortas avenged him.

The ancient acropolis crowned the summit of the Ithome whilst the surrounding wall was 9 kilometres in circumference.

We must cross the village in order to visit the museum, and, on descending by a path on the left towards the centre of the old town, we can discern the remains of a theatre as well as of a vast terrace on which are the ruins of a large temple. It was perhaps the Hierothysion which contained statues of all the known Greek gods, as well as a bronze effigy of Epaminondas. The nearby *agora* was lined with porticoes. To the south, there were some important buildings including a theatre with an orchestra paved with coloured marble, a *propylon* and the *Synedrion* which was the meeting place of the Messenian Assembly.

To the south near the *heroon*, excavations have brought to light a building with an inner courtyard surrounded with colonnades which was perhaps the Prytanaeum, and to the north-west, an *exedra* situated in front of a portico of the second half of the 4th century B.C.

There are many other remains of ancient buildings on this site, including the Arsinoe fountain on the *agora*, the scanty vestiges of the stadium and the barely discernible traces of temples and of tombs.

We continue towards the Gate of Arcady or of Megalopolis, one of the most perfect examples of Greek fortifications of the 4th century, together with the adjacent sector of the ramparts.

This gate, which is reached by a paved way, consists of two entrances, separated by a round courtyard. The inner gate is covered by an enormous monolithic lintel, broken in two places, and leaning on one of the supports of the door. The court was surrounded by a massive Hellenic wall built without mortar but with such perfect masonry that the joints can scarcely be seen. Two niches on each side held the tutelary gods, one of whom was doubtless the stone Hermes mentioned by Pausanias. The outer gate was flanked with two massive square towers of which only the foundations remain.

To the east and to the west is the splendid wall which climbs up the slope of the Ithome, and the western crests with the facings of square blocks of stone. The scarpments which prevented the approach of war machines compensated for the low height of the ramparts which were only 4·57 metres at this point. They did, however, have defenders armed with the long Doric lance, and marksmen to keep assailants at bay.

The ramparts are flanked at irregular intervals which vary from 30 to 40 metres with square towers built astride the walls. They were two-storeyed with windows and arrow slits, and in places, some small posterns on the ground floor.

Forty metres from the gate, it is possible to visit a tower

which is almost intact although shaken by an earthquake. A staircase leads from the interior of the city to the platform that surmounts the whole circuit of the walls. From the village, the climb to the summit of Ithome takes forty minutes. First of all we come upon the remains of the aqueduct that supplied the Clepsydra fountain which has disappeared, then on a terrace surrounded by supporting walls we see the vestiges of a small Ionian temple which was dedicated to Artemis Laphria.

On the summit of Ithome, the ancient monastery of Vourkano, which was built prior to the 16th century, is flanked by a campanile. The main gate, surmounted by a coat of arms, opens on to a paved courtyard surrounded by abandoned buildings, with a chapel on the left. This monastery occupies the site of the sanctuary of Zeus Ithomatas. It was not a temple, but a simple altar where human sacrifices were sometimes made, so it is here that Aristodemos sacrificed his daughter. It was here also that the annual feast of the Ithomae was celebrated and to this day the tradition survives in a panegyric.

The first statue of the god, a work of the Argian sculptor Hageladas, was brought back from Naupaetus where the Messenians had emigrated in order to place themselves under the protection of Athens in 370 B.C. The sanctuary was a place of asylum for slaves whom the priest could enfranchise.

Besides the sanctuary there was, on the summit of Ithome, the ancient fortress which served as a place of refuge to the Messenians during the last two Messenian wars.

From the summit there is a magnificent view over Mount Taygetus, the two plains of Messenia, the sources of the Pamisos, Mount Hellenitsa and Erymanthe as well as across the coast of Elis and as far as the island of Zante.

We shall be able to descend to the gate of Laconia in half an hour. It was built on a pass which separates the Ithome from Mount Eva which was consecrated to Dionysos and to the Evades Bacchantes.

We now rejoin the Megalopolis road by passing through MELIGALA, the largest town of upper Messenia. It was the capital of the first Doric dynasty in Messenia, that of Kresphonte in the 12th century B.C.

Twenty metres to the west of the village, is the old triple bridge of Mavrozoumenos. It is composed of three arms radiating from a large central pier above the marshy confluence of Leucasia and of Emphitos at the junction of the roads of Messena, of Phigalia, and of Megalopolis. The apron, the arches and the actual spurs date from the Turkish régime, whilst the bases of the central pier and of the other piers are Hellenic. There were seven vaulted and corbelled arches and a small lateral passage covered with a flat roof and going in a south-west direction.

Now we shall reach the top of the Makri-Plaghi Pass, the chief means of access of communication between Messenia and Arcadia. From the village of Paradisia, at the far end of the pass, a four hours' walk will take us to the ruins of the medieval fortress of KALIKALA on the site of *Ampheia* of the Ancients.

One of the churches at Kokkala is the sanctuary of Phaneromi in the Chronicle of Morea.

Soon we shall cross the Alphea and come to MEGALOPOLIS, a big modern township situated not far from the ruins of the old town, which we can find by taking the road to Pyrgos and from there the path which leads to the cemetery.

The Great Town, as the Greeks called it, which the Romans christened Megalopolis, was built in four years from 371–368 by the orders of Epaminondas to be the capital of united Arcadia and to keep Sparta in check.

The inhabitants of forty Arcadian townships and a number of citizens from the larger cities were transported to newly-constructed Megalopolis. Here the Arcadian Confederation had a Senate and an Assembly, known as the Assembly of the Ten Thousand, which sat in the Thersilion, whilst the executive power was in the hands of the *strategus* supported by a federal troop of 500 *eparites*. Discord soon broke out and the countrymen began to regret their villages. Besieged and ravaged several times, the Great City was more or less abandoned and then rebuilt in 194. By the time Pausanias came here it was nothing more than a heap of ruins. Under the last emperors, Megalopolis became an episcopal see, and it was last mentioned in the 7th century; after the Slav invasions it disappeared from notice.

The theatre is built on the side of a hill and is the largest of the whole of Greece, for it could contain 20,000 spectators. Since it is surrounded by trees, it makes a very attractive feature of the landscape.

To the right, opposite the tiers, the *parados* was occupied by a long rectangular building which contained the wardrobe of the performers. In the 4th century, the stage was made of wood and could be dismantled so that between performances the material could be deposited in this wardrobe building.

Behind the stage, a short stairway led to a projecting portico which communicated with the vast square building of the *Thersilion*, the seat of the Federal Assembly of the Ten Thousand. It could accommodate 6,000 seated members and 10,000 standing, and it was laid out like an odeon with circular tiers and the tribune in the centre.

In this region large altars have been found as well as the site of the stadium and the sanctuaries of Dionysus and Aesculapius.

The town, which was built on the plain on both banks of the Helisson, had a wall 8,850 metres in circumference and built of sun-baked bricks on a foundation of masonry; it was flanked with round and square towers of which only scanty vestiges remain. The river divided the town into two quarters which were connected by a bridge. The theatre was in the federal city, whilst the municipal city was on the other bank.

On setting off by the Pyrgos road, we shall see on the right, after having crossed the Helisson, the site of the *agora* which was the precinct of the Great Sanctuary of Zeus Soter. A vast rectangular structure rose in the middle of the court and the temple occupied the far wing.

To the east of the *agora* was the portico of Myopolis, the scent market built by the tyrant Aristodemos towards 250. To the west stood the triple-colonnaded portico of Philip.

We shall continue our way along the Pyrgos road which may be completed and asphalted by the time this book appears. In any case, it is essential to see the temple of Bassae which is one of the most harmonious and best preserved in the whole of Greece; already the road from Andritsena to Bassae is finished.

We shall pass near the picturesque village of KARYTAINA whose white houses are laid out in tiers on the slopes of a hill which has, on its summit, a powerful Frankish castle built in 1254 on an astonishing rocky peak almost surrounded by a deep gorge.

If there is not time to visit the ruins of the castle, it is at least possible to inspect them from the road which runs along the far side of the ravine in which the Alphi flows. Those who wish to do so, can take the road to the village and from there continue along a track on foot.

Karytaina stands on the site of the ancient *Brenthe* which served as a place of refuge to the population of Gortys when they were driven back by the Slavs. In 1209 the Franks made Karytaina the capital of a large barony which comprised 22 fiefs. It was allotted to Hughes de Bruyères who built the castle. His son, Geoffroy I de Bruyères was the Sire de Karytaina celebrated in the Chronicle of Morea as the paragon of knighthood. In 1320 Karytaina was bought by the Emperor Andronicus II Paleologue. We shall find first of all at the lower end of the village, two churches, of which the more interesting, the Panaghia, dates from the 11th century. It is flanked by a Frankish belfry and, in the interior, there are some ancient pictures and a coat of arms of the Albamonte.

Then from the village a ten minutes' walk along a path leads to the only gateway of the castle, which is a typical example of the Frankish fortifications in the Morea.

The approach ramp passes through two lines of ramparts and terminates at the ruins of a bastion known as the "House of Kalotronis" with a little church of Haghia Andreas. Retracing our steps, we climb to the entrance of the *kastro*, crossing first of all a small courtyard and passing under a gateway defended by a tower and by battlements. Continuing by a vaulted passage and crossing the courtyard, we shall come to a great reception wing above a vaulted cistern.

The Frankish *enceinte*, triangular in plan, is terminated to the north by a circular bastion. Its parapets have been adapted for artillery and musket fire.

On leaving Karytaina, we can go to the ruins of the ancient *Gortys* of Arcadia which is of interest only to archaeologists. At the end of two hours' walking we shall find, not far from the confluence of the Gortynios and the Alpheos, the remains of two sanctuaries consecrated to Aesculapius and of a thermal establishment.

The Temple of Asclepios on the banks of the Gortynios and to the west of the chapel of Aghios Andreas, comprised a *pronaos in antis* and a *cella*, but no *opisthodome*. It was begun towards the middle of the 4th century B.C., but it was not completed, for the stones of the foundation were used for a reconstruction of the thermal establishment which was built to the south towards the end of the 4th century and remodelled towards the middle of the 3rd century.

Then we find the ruins of a Roman building and, in an olive grove, the vestiges of a small *cella*, the remains of a portico of the 4th century B.C. and then some human dwellings, etc.

The whole site was defended by two *enceintes*, the first, the *enceinte* of the Acropolis, had three gateways; another to the south was rather smaller in diameter. The second temple, to the south-west of the Acropolis, and very much ruined, dates from the end of the 5th century B.C.

The road, still undulating, continues to ANDRITSAINA, a little township full of charm, built on the slopes of the mountain with picturesque wooden houses, and a good hotel, the Xenia.

From this place it is possible to make the ascent of Mount Lyceus where, according to legend, Rhea secretly gave birth to Zeus. There is also an excellent asphalted road which winds up the side of the mountain to the edge of a narrow deserted plain and the splendid TEMPLE OF BASSAE. This building stands in a place of nostalgic solitude among a few scattered oak trees.

Dedicated to Apollo Epikouios, it was probably built, at the time of a plague which ravaged the Peloponnesus, by the architect Ictinos who designed the Parthenon. The construction was paid for by the Phygalians as a thanksgiving to Apollo for having saved them from the plague.

The temple was discovered in 1765 by the Frenchman Bocher and in 1811 the Society for the Dilettanti explored the site and detached from the monument carvings which are now in the British Museum.

Ictinos made use of the three orders in the construction of the Temple of Apollo built of local limestone. The 6 slender and graceful columns of the façade and the 15 flanking columns are of the Ionic order and fluted.

Contrary to the usual practice, the *pronaos* lies to the north of the main structure. From there a door opens on to the *cella*, whose rear portion, which is the longest, is lined on each side by two rows of five Ionic columns. The frieze, which ran along the walls, represented combats between Greeks and Amazons, Centaurs and Lapiths. The two last abutments on the south are arranged obliquely so as to free the rear part where the limits are marked by an isolated Corinthian column which is the oldest specimen of this order. The rear part of the *cella* formed the sanctuary with the statue of the god which backed against the west wall, facing the lateral door opening out towards the east.

The arrangement re-established the normal orientation of the primitive sanctuary. It was the configuration of the land which had imposed the orientation from north to south. Since there is no sign of a plinth on the paving, the statue was doubtless made of wood, for the great bronze statue mentioned by Pausanias stood outside the temple on a huge pedestal. Later it was transported to Megalopolis and replaced by one of marble.

Seventy metres to the west, the foundation of a complex of Archaic and Classical buildings have been laid bare.

We must now return to Andritsaina. This place can serve as a centre for a number of different excursions which we will mention briefly. First there is Mount Lyceus which takes three hours and a quarter to climb, but must be done with a guide.

Then to the north, there is the ancient *Alipheira* with the foundations of two temples and a funerary edifice, two hours away on foot.

From Bassae itself, a walk of two or three hours will take us to ancient *Phygalia,* which has conserved some remains of its ramparts and the foundations of several temples.

From Andritsaina we will continue on our way to Pyrgos. The first village to be seen on the left on the heights is dominated by the acropolis of the ancient *Aepion* which still has the ruins of a theatre and the remains of its ramparts.

Next we will go to Krestaena. One can see in the neighbourhood the picturesque ruins of the Gothic monastery of Our Lady of Issova, known as *Palatia,* built by the Franks and burnt down by the Greeks in 1264.

Further on, a track to the right leads to the village of Makrysia, 2 kilometres away, situated near the ancient *Scil-*

lonte where the vestiges of a Doric temple have been discovered. It may have been the Temple of Athena Skilountis, or the one which Xenophon had erected on his lands on the model of the Artemision of Ephesus.

Not far from there, on the plateau of Babes, a little Doric temple of the beginning of the 5th century B.C. has been discovered, as well as vestiges of houses of the same epoch.

We next come to PYRGOS which is a modern town on the site of the ancient *Latrines*, situated on the Sacred Way from Elis to Olympia. It has preserved nothing of its past and offers nothing of interest to the tourist.

OLYMPIA is only 23 kilometres away by a really excellent road. Olympia attracts us by the peaceful harmony of a landscape full of charm where the silvery waters of the River Alpheus ripple over their bed of sand among the trees and wooded hills.

It was never a town, but a vast sanctuary where the temples and altars dedicated to the different deities were assembled under the protection of Zeus, and of the city of Pisa first, and Elis after 471 B.C. Thousands came from all parts of the Greek World to attend the celebrations of the most ancient and venerated worship of Hellas. The *sacred truce* would for the time being put an end to all discord.

Before the 6th century, most of the temples were on the southern slopes of Mount Kronon, and near to the terrace with the treasury could be seen the Pritanaeum, the Heraion, the Hippodaeion, the Pelopeion, the Great Temple of Zeus, the Theokoleon, numerous shrines, altars and votive monuments, the Stadium and the Hippodrome. After the 4th century B.C., the Barbarians began to send offerings: Philip of Macedon ordered the Philippeion to be built, and it is in this period that the Leonidaion, the Palestra, the Gymnasium, the Portico, and the Metroon were erected. But under the Roman domination the decline continued, and so the quinquennial festival was held for the last time in A.D. 393. In A.D. 426,

Theodosius ordered the destruction of the pagan temples, and towards the middle of the 6th century the ruins that remained were overturned.

A Byzantine city was built in the middle of the ruins, and a church was erected on the site of the workshop of Phidias. Then the Kladeos burst its ancient dykes, and landslides from Mount Kronon swept over the Terrace of the Treasures so that the Byzantine city disappeared and was replaced by a humble hamlet of shepherds with houses scattered between the Stadium and the Temple of Zeus. Finally the mud from the river floods and the mud washed down the mountainside combined to cover the ruins with a layer of earth and rubble from 3 to 6 metres thick.

The visit to this site begins with the Gymnasium of the Hellenistic era which is composed of two long porticoes on each side of a vast square. The eastern portico, which has not been completely uncovered, was 210 metres long and was used for training athletes in bad weather. It is composed of a double gallery of an inner colonnade and a lateral colonnade, both of them Doric. The long wall at the back built on foundations of tufa, was supported on the outer side by embankments. The southern portico, whose far end has been washed away by the river, is a simple gallery with a Doric colonnade. It communicated with a basin and, at the junction of the two *xystes*, a monumental gateway provided access to the street.

Next we come to the ruins of the Palestra of the end of the 3rd century B.C. It was the part of the gymnasium used for wrestling and there were special rooms where the wrestlers could anoint themselves with oil and bathe. The gymnasium was composed of great galleries, *xystes*, and tracks for racing on foot around a huge courtyard for collective games and exercises. In the Palestra and the Gymnasium of Olympia, the wrestlers and runners completed, during their last month under the supervision of the Hellanodices, the training which had lasted nine months in the gymnasium of Elis. The palestra of Olympia had a central courtyard with peristyles bordered one side by a quadruple portico of fluted Doric columns. The galleries of the peristyle provided access to closed or open rooms.

Further to the south, during the Roman domination, a large house with a central courtyard was built on the ruins of the Theokoleon where the priests were lodged.

To the west can be seen the ruins of a *heroon*, that is to say the chapel of a dead man who has been acclaimed a hero. A colonnade led to a vestibule and on into a square courtyard in which was built a rotunda.

Further to the west, near to the bed of the Kladeos, are the ruins of several thermes dating from the 5th century B.C. to the Roman epoch.

Next can be seen, to the south of the Theokoleon and the *heroon*, the remains of the workshop of Phidias which was destined for the life-size maquettes of the statue of Zeus. Built in the 5th century B.C., it was transformed into a church in the Byzantine era.

To the south, a vast edifice, the Leonidaion, erected towards the end of the 3rd century B.C. by the Naxian Leonidas, was used as a hostel and to receive guests of importance. It is the largest structure in Olympia. The atrium in the centre with its impluvium was lined by a Doric peristyle of 44 columns which was faced by a number of apartments surrounded by a belt of exterior galleries forming a quadrangular line of 138 Ionic columns.

After passing the ruins of a thermal complex of the 3rd century A.D., we will come to the ruins of the *bouleuterion*, or Palace of the Olympic Senate, where the competitors took an oath to observe the rules of the game in the presence of the Hellanodices.

It was composed of a great Ionic portico and of a square central area flanked by two long wings that ended in apses.

The statue of Zeus Horklos stood in the centre of this open

square, and in the post-Roman period, a courtyard with a Doric peristyle was added to the portico of the façade.

To the south of the *bouleuterion*, a long gallery called the Southern Portico, dates from the 4th century B.C., but was remodelled during the Roman domination.

The *bouleuterion* stood on the edge of the Roman wall of the Altis which limited the sacred part of Olympia where stood the sanctuaries. The *enceinte* of the Hellenic period was smaller.

The Temple of Zeus, which we will next see, was the richest and largest of the Altis. It stood on an immense foundation which still exists. Surrounding this are the enormous drums of columns which show the huge size of the construction. It was built by the Elean architect, Libon, who was financed by the booty taken by the Eleans from the Pisates in 468, but it was perhaps remodelled at the time of the installation of the huge statue in gold and ivory by Phidias, and then again towards the middle of the 4th century B.C.

It was a Doric temple, peripteral and hexastyle. A stylobate in conchitic stone and with three steps was built on a foundation of tufa. A ramp and lateral staircases led to the peristyle which had 13 columns on one side, and 6 on the façade. The drums and capitals of these columns are covered with a stucco made from the dust of white marble. We may assume that the capitals, pediments and architraves were decorated with palmettes and painted mouldings. The marble mouldings were decorated with lions' masks. The beams of the roof were of wood, but the tiles and the joists were of Naxos marble. Important fragments of the pediments are on display in the museum. The eastern pediment represented the preparations for the contest between Pelops and Oenomaus. The last Aetolian King of Elis had been told by an oracle that he would be killed by his son-in-law, so he insisted that all the suitors of his daughter Hippodamia should out-distance him in a chariot race in which the loser would forfeit his life.

The King had a pair of mares of outstanding swiftness and thirteen suitors had already suffered the penalty of death when Pelops, chief of the Achaeans, presented himself. Pelops bribed the King's driver Myrtilos to take out the linchpin of his master's chariot and so won the race and the bride. According to another version, Pelops cast a spell on the King's horses so that they bolted and fell into a ravine. The victorious Pelops pierced the King with his lance and took over his realm.

In the centre of the pediment, Zeus appears with bared chest, with his robes falling over his hips and legs. To the left can be seen Oenomaus, his wife Sterope, and a maid-servant kneeling in front of the chariot horses, an old man who is doubtless the oracle, a crouching slave and the recumbent allegoric figure of Kladeos. To the right of Zeus stands Pelops with a helmet on his head, with Hippodamia in a long tunic reaching to the ground, a slave in front of the chariot, the driver of Oenomaus, and the recumbent figure of Alpheus.

The other pediment represents the combat between the Lapiths and the Centaurs at the bridal feast of Pirithoos. The Centaurs became drunk and tried to carry off the women and the young boys when a battle ensued. Thus the Centaur Eurythion can be seen attacking Deidamia whilst Pirithoos attacks him with a knife. A Lapith woman kneels with torn tunic whilst trying to escape from a Centaur whom a kneeling Lapith transpierces with his sword. An old slave woman leans on a cushion and watches the fighting together with a Thessalian nymph lying down in one corner.

On the left hand side can be seen, to the right of Apollo, a Centaur seizing a young Lapith woman, whilst someone who must be Theseus strikes him with an axe. Next, a young Centaur strikes down a young Lapith boy whose arm he bites, and nearby a Lapith girl kneels whilst a Centaur grasps her hair just as a Lapith knocks him down. Behind two recumbent women a nymph stands with bared breast.

The frieze of the peristyle in the *cella* was decorated with *metopes* illustrating the Labours of Hercules. Three of them are in the Louvre and represented in the Museum of Olympia by mouldings. The others are more or less mutilated.

The entablatures were adorned with bronze statues, votive offerings and decorated with golden shields and the *acroteria* were formed of gilded basins on tripods.

The *pronaos* was closed by a triple grille, and the *cella* was divided into three aisles by a double row of seven Doric columns that supported two galleries of the first floor, and an upper colonnade which supported the wooden ceiling. Lateral staircases led to the upper gallery from which visitors could inspect the head of the statue of Zeus by Phidias.

This chryselephantine statue which Phidias had produced in collaboration with Panainos, the painter, and Colotes, the metal worker, was from 12 to 13 metres high. The god was seated, holding a *Victory* in chryselephantine in his right hand, in the left a sceptre surmounted by an eagle. The throne of oak and bronze was sheathed in ivory and special servants were entrusted with the task of oiling the exterior. Theodosius II carried it off to Constantinople where it was destroyed by a fire in A.D. 475.

The plinths of numerous statues were placed on the ramp leading to the temple; these were Olympian statues, and the chariots dedicated to them.

On leaving this place, you will see to the south-east of the Wall of Altis, the ruins of several buildings, of which one was a vast villa erected by the orders of Nero so that he could have somewhere to stay in Olympia. On the façade there was a colonnade of 19 Doric columns, and the residence also had two lateral colonnades of 8 columns.

To the east of this mansion, there was the entrance of the Hippodrome which was washed away by the floods of the Alpheus, and between this entrance and the entrance of the Stadium there was a portico called the *Portico of the Echo* or *of Poecile* which opened directly on to the Altis. It was named thus because sounds were echoed seven times, and also because of the paintings which decorated the ceiling. This portico was built in the second half of the 4th century B.C., and a long stylobate preceded by three steps supported the 44 Doric columns. The covered walk inside was divided into two galleries by a central colonnade of 21 Ionic columns.

Next we penetrate the stadium of the Olympic Games by a covered walk of the 1st century B.C. which was used by the competitors. The greater part of the running track has been cleared, and the starting point and the finish are discernible.

This stadium could hold 20,000 spectators, though tiers of seats were only hollowed out of the earth towards the end of the Roman era.

To the right of the entrance of the stadium there is a terrace, part of which was occupied by a series of treasuries dedicated in the 6th and 5th centuries B.C. by different Greek nations, more especially from Sicily and Magna Graecia. The ruins of 13 of these structures have been laid bare.

Below can be seen the bases of the statues of the Zabes, bronze statues of Zeus which the people of Elis paid for with the fines inflicted by the Hallanodices. Nearby is the Metroon, or Temple of the Mother of the Gods, or of Rhea Cybele, which was transformed later on into a Temple of Augustus and of the Roman Emperors whose statues were to be found in the *cella*.

It was a peripteral Doric temple *in antis*, with 7 columns on the façades and 11 on each side.

To the west of the Metroon, excavations have brought to light a complex of six prehistoric houses with rectangular rooms terminating in an apse. The vestiges of two of these dwellings can be seen opposite the ruins of the *exedra* of Herodes Atticus. This structure was built between A.D. 157 and 160. It comprises a large rectangular basin flanked with small rotundas, each of which contained a fountain, whilst there were 15 niches with statues.

Near to this spot are the remains of the *Heraion* or Temple of Hera, which is one of the oldest Doric temples known. It was built towards the end of the 7th century B.C. by the inhabitants of Scillonte. In the *cella* were found the plinth and the copy, if not the original, of the Hermes of Praxiteles which is in the Museum of Olympia.

It was a peripteral temple with 6 columns in front and 13 at the sides. Their diameter and their style differ so that their capitals vary from the Archaic cushion type to the elaborate Roman capitals with straight echinas and the unobtrusive ones of the 5th century.

In the *cella*, the columns did not stand out from the walls, but were in couples in the form of pilasters whose projections divided each side of the *cella* into five chapels. There were statues in these chapels; the first one on the right was the setting for the Hermes of Praxiteles and the statue of a Roman ivory.

The *opisthodome* did not communicate with the *cella*, but only with the peristyle; in it was deposited the famous casket offered by Cypselos, Tyrant of Corinth. It was made in the 6th century of carved wood, but with plating of gold and of ivory.

In this Temple of Hera there were no sculptures in the pediments and no *metopes*, for the plastic decoration was reduced to mouldings and gutters of painted terracotta.

To the south of the Heraion, beyond a high altar, the remains of a pentagonal *enceinte* surround a small hillock to form a sacred enclosure which was dedicated by the Achaians of Pisa to Pelops, so that it is one of the oldest monuments of the Altis. In the centre was the altar dedicated to the hero, as well as his statue and a ditch in which black rams were sacrificed.

Standing between the Heraion and the Palestra, the *Philip-*

peion was a circular edifice begun by Philip II of Macedon and completed by Alexander the Great. The centre of the *cella* was occupied by a great stone base on which stood five chryselephantine statues by Leochares: there was an effigy of Philip between those of Amyntae, his father, Eurydice, his mother, on the right, and those of Alexander and of Olympias, wife of Philip, on the left.

There still subsist the ruins of the *pritanaeum* of the 5th century B.C., with to the south of the Chapel of Hestia, and to the north, the Hestiatoion, a huge dining-room where the guests of honour and the victors in the games were fed during the Festival, and where the priests and the officials usually took their meals.

Finally we should visit the museum which contains all the objects and statues found in the course of excavations, besides the pediments and *metopes* of the Temple of Zeus which we have already mentioned, the Victory of Paeonios which stood in the Temple of Zeus, the group of Zeus carrying off Ganymede and other sculptures of outstanding interest such as the treasure of Megara.

From Olympia we must return to Pyrgos, and from there we may go on directly to Patras or else take the road towards Loutra Kaiafa and pass through SAMIKON, which is in a lovely valley. It was celebrated for its Temple of Poseidon Samian. The ruins are on one of the foothills of Mount Lapithas and here we can see the remains of the city wall of which the oldest parts of the 6th century B.C. are constructed of dressed masonry. The entrance to the fortress is by a gate facing south. The sanctuary of Poseidon was on one of the three mounds which were formerly protected by a wall.

LOUTRA KAIAFA is a thermal resort with springs flowing out of a great cave which may have been the grotto of the Anidrides Nymphs where the Ancients came to treat their skin diseases. The River Anidros which issued from these springs possessed the same properties and flowed into a fetid marsh where the fish were considered to be uneatable. The sulphurous waters of Loutra Kaiafa are said to be efficient for the treatment of chronic eczema, neuritis and chronic catarrh.

Returning once more to Pyrgos, we can continue on our way to KATAKOLON, a little port where can be seen on the isthmus the ruins of the fort of Katakolon or Pondiko Kastro, which was the Beauvoir of the Villehardouins. To the west, near Cape *Pheia*, the town of the same name was swallowed up in the 6th century B.C. by the earthquake that overturned the Temple of Zeus at Olympia.

Next we must take the road to Patras, crossing the Iardanos, the Homeric river whose Phoenician name is the Jordan. And it was near to this stream that the Pylians of Nestor fought against the Arcadians.

Thirteen kilometres further on, a road on the left leads to the beach of Kourota and soon we shall reach the big township of GASTOUNI, the ancient residence of the Frankish princes of Achaia, and known to them as Gastogne. By taking a little road to the left, we can visit a charming and well-preserved Byzantine church of the 10th century.

Next we come to ANDRAVIDA village, the former capital of the Frankish princes of Morea under the name of Andreville. Before leaving this town, we shall find, also on our left and about 100 metres from the road, a little Gothic cathedral built by the Franks; known as St. Sophia, it was the metropolitan church of the Latin bishops until the 15th century. The nave is in ruins, but the choir is still standing.

The princes of Morea often summoned assemblies and parliaments of the Frankish barons at Andreville. The Templars built the church of St. James where were buried Geoffroy I, Geoffroy II and Guillaume de Villehardouin, but no vestige of this building remains, nor indeed of the Church of St. Nicolas nor of the monastery of St. Nicolas of Carmel.

We next take the road leading to Kyllini, but half-way there we take the highway signposted *Kastro*, which is wide, stone-covered, and even asphalted in places: it goes straight to the Frankish Castle of CHLEMOUTSI which we have seen rising up on the horizon on a round and isolated hill which dominates the whole peninsula.

This castle, which can be reached from the village by a road which has just been laid, was built by the Franks in 1220–1223. It was later taken over by the Venetians who named it Castel Tornese, but they were replaced by a Catalan company under Ferdinand of Majorca who captured it in 1314 and kept it for two years. Constantine Paleologue captured it in 1427 and then dismantled it, but later the Turks restored the entire fortress and adapted it for artillery and musketry fire.

It is composed of a more or less oval ring of battlemented ramparts with a hexagonal keep in the centre. It is preceded by a lower courtyard surrounded by a curtain wall and with a round tower in the centre, but the wall is pierced by the main gateway of the castle. Both the tower and the curtain were built by the Turks.

The keep is in the south-west of the central court which is surrounded by high, wide galleries that are partially ruined, and the chapel has been made in the northern gallery.

All this is on a large scale, but rather desolate, for yawning gaps mark the places which have been stripped of their stonework. We must regret that, just as at Methoni, this masterpiece of military architecture should have been so completely abandoned and left to decay. Careful restoration and maintenance would turn these fortresses into real attractions for the tourist.

From Chlemoutsi we can continue to KYLLINI. It is the Clair-Mont of the French and Carentza or Glarentza of the Venetians. There is a service of steamers from this port to the Island of Zante.

Kyllini, the ancient *Cyllene*, is not far from the Homeric city of *Hyrmine*, and it is a port for merchant shipping. In the Middle Ages, it became a fortified city, one of the favourite residences of the Villehardouins, Princes of Achaia, and then of the Angevins whose luxurious court is described in the Chronicle of Morea. The Venetian or Genoese ships sailing from Brindisi or Taranto used Kyllini as a port of call.

Only scanty vestiges of the ramparts, the towers and the churches remain of the medieval city which extended over the plateau near Kyllini, and the ruins of the Castle were dynamited during the Second World War. The most perceptible ruins are those of a large church built on the same plan as St. Sophia of Andravida.

After leaving Kyllini, we must continue on our way to Patras. At Vardas a road on the left leads to *Manoillade* of the Franks, whilst we go on to Kato Achaia, the capital of the Deme of Dyme, a city founded by the Epeans, and later the seat of an important Roman colony established in the reign of Augustus.

According to tradition, Guillaume de Champlitte landed on this coast on May 1st, 1206, having come to Greece with a Venetian fleet in order to conquer the Morea, though the first landing was made in 1204 near Methoni.

From the road which now skirts the Gulf of Patras there are extensive prospects of the coast of Aetolia.

PATRAS, on the site of the ancient *Patrae*, is an important commercial city and port, and third in population of the whole of Greece. The old Acropolis is crowned by the ruins of a Byzantine castle which was restored in turn by the Franks, the Venetians and the Turks.

We will enter this citadel by the Haghios Nicolaos street. It is composed of an inner keep and of ramparts and a gate opening through a large tower of the Turkish period, with an ancient ruined gateway to the north, and heptagonal Turkish tower at the south-east angle. This wall is full of masonry of the Hellenistic age and of the Byzantine epoch. To the east and to the south, the curtains were built by the Franks whilst the Venetians were responsible for a circular bastion at the western angle, and the Paleologues for the many-sided towers.

At the summit of the old Acropolis, the keep is separated from the outer wall by an outwork and a shallow ditch spanned by a bridge. It was reinforced by the Paleologues who built a bastion at the projecting corner of the keep, whilst a big supporting bastion with slanting sides was erected by the Venetians.

Next we should take Haghiou Georgiou Street so as to visit the odeon which was built during the Roman domination and destroyed in the 3rd century A.D. The proscenium wall has been rebuilt together with its niches and doors.

Finally, the archaeological museum contains a few important pieces of sculpture and a whole series of vases.

The excellent restaurant of the Evagelatos Brothers at 9 St. Nicholas Street serves grilled crabs, octopus stewed in their own ink, lamb stewed with artichokes and grilled lamb.

At RHION we will find the landing stage of the Rhion Andirrhion ferry which crosses the narrows of the Gulf of Corinth in 15 minutes. People who have already visited Delphi and wish to go on to Macedonia are not advised to continue the rest of this Peloponnesus circuit to Corinth, for this part of the itinerary is of no particular interest as far as monuments are concerned.

At Rhion, near the landing stage, there is a fairly well-preserved fortress known as the Castle of Morea and built by Sultan Bajazet II before he set out to conquer the Morea in 1499.

On the other side of the Bay, there is another small Turkish fort.

Next we should go to AEGION, a slightly larger port where it is possible to embark on the ferry to Itea and from there it is easy to drive up to Delphi.

Aegion evokes the name of the goat that suckled Zeus but,

as some may remember, it was one of the twelve cities of the Achaean League, and it was here that Agamemnon assembled the chieftains of Greece before setting out for Troy. After the destruction of Helike in 373 B.C., Aegion became the capital of Achaia, and harboured a sanctuary where the assemblies of the Achaian League were held.

During the Byzantine era, it was given the Slav name of Vostitsa and, in 1209, at the time of the partition of the Morea, Geoffroy de Villehardouin granted the fief of the barony of Vostice to Sir Hugues de Charpigny.

Near the springs which still flow in the lower town could be found the sacred wood and the Homarion which was the federal sanctuary of Zeus Homarios. All that remains of the old town are vestiges of the ramparts and underground rooms carved out of the solid rock.

Next we should go to Diakopton which can be reached by train in 55 minutes, and from there a walk of an hour and twenty-five minutes will take us to MEGASPILAION. The cog railway passes through the Gap of Vournnikos, hemmed in first of all between two precipitous slopes, and then between pine-clad hills. Viaducts span the foaming torrent that forces its way between the scattered rocks. A fairly steep climb leads to the Megaspilaion, the "Great Grotto" which takes its name from the deep cleft which conceals within its depths the monastic buildings. An imposing white façade flanked with a corner tower displays buildings seven or eight storeys high, with dormer windows, loggia and galleries. There is a taverna on a tree-shaded terrace where visitors may have meals and refreshments.

According to an old legend, a shepherdess of Imperial stock living at Zachlorou discovered an image of the Virgin which was believed to have miraculous virtues. The Monastery of the Assumption of the Blessed Virgin Mary was founded by Constantine Paleologue. There were repeated fires, and in the year 1400 an admirable library containing rare manuscripts was destroyed. The church was rebuilt in 1641 and decorated with frescoes in 1653. It is on the first floor, and its door is decorated with silver-plated copper relief work. It contains numerous votive offerings and relics. A niche protected by a shutter of moulded silver, with paintings by Raoul Paleologue, contains a miraculous wax ikon of the Virgin and Child. It is a rather clumsy work of the 8th or 9th century and is attributed, naturally enough, to St. Luke.

The refectory, the cells and the kitchen can be visited.

By chartering a guide, a walk of more than six hours will take you to the falls of the Styx, a river that does not deserve its legendary reputation.

From Diakopton we must continue along the coast, skirting first of all a fine beach and coming to the village of Mavra Litharia situated on a plain covered with olive trees and near to the site of an ancient port. Next we will pass through the seaside resorts of Dermeni and Xylocastron, and on to Kiaton and, after crossing the village of Sikyonia, we shall come to the ruins of Sicyon, 6 kilometres from the Corinth-Patras road. This city was founded in the second millennium by the Ionians and then conquered by the Dorians.

Under the pacific tyranny of the Otharides (650–570 B.C.) it was the centre of a brillant school of wax painting with Eupompos, Pamphilos and Pausias, and of sculpture with Aristocles, Kleoetas and Canachos.

Sicyon suffered during the conflicts between the aristocrats and the democrats and was finally subdued by Epaminondas in 368. Destroyed by Demetrios Poliocretes in 303, it was rebuilt and took the name of Demetrias. Though the city was popular with the Romans, its fortunes continued to decline until at last an earthquake completed its ruin. The museum is in partially-restored Roman baths and contains vases of the Archaic period found at Stymphalos, including also vases with red and black figures, some sculptures and some terracotta figurines.

Sicyon is situated on an immense plateau of reddish earth and fertile land where the vines alternate with fields of wheat, tobacco plantations, olive groves and orange and lemon orchards with here and there the contrast of a black cypress. From the top of the acropolis where the goats graze, there is a prospect of what remains of the ancient city, both Hellenistic and Roman. There remains nothing of the temples described by Pausanias and only the gymnasium and the theatre are fairly well-preserved, though the theatre is sometimes used for theatrical or operatic performances.

A single column remains standing below the acropolis. It was part of the gymnasium of Clinias where the rooms reserved for the athletes can still be seen and, against the lower terrace, the remains of the two fountains between the three staircases which led to the upper part, of the Roman period. It is also possible to recognize the site of the ancient *agora*, the great square of the *bouleuterion*, the Council Chamber, the foundations of the corresponding portico on the left, and those of a little temple which may have been dedicated to Artemis.

After leaving the coast, the road passes in front of the ruins of the Basilica of Lechaion of which we have already spoken.

Our tour of the Peloponnesus will come to an end soon after, when we reach Corinth.

GLOSSARY

Abacus : Flat slab on top of a capital.

Abutment : Solid masonry placed to resist the lateral pressure of a vault.

Acanthus : Plant with thick fleshy and scalloped leaves copied as part of decoration of a Corinthian capital and in some types of leaf-carving.

Acroterion : Pedestal for a statue at the angle of the pediment.

Adyton : Inner sanctuary.

Aedicule : Small structure sheltering altar or image of household god; small pedimented structure over a niche.

Agora : Market Place.

Aleipterion : Chamber for athletes' anointing at gymnasia.

Anta : A pilaster terminating the side wall of a Greek temple with the base and capital differing from those of adjacent columns.

Ambulatory : Open or covered arcade or cloister; an aisle around a choir.

Antiphonary : Book of chants or anthems.

Apse : Eastern end of church containing Bishop's Throne.

Apsidiole : Secondary apse.

Arcade : Range of arches supported on piers or columns, freestanding. Blind Arcade : Arcade set against a wall.

Arcature : Blind arcade.

Architrave : Lowest division of entablature rising on capitals of supporting column. Collective name for various parts surrounding a door or window.

Archivolt : Moulding curving round the under surface of an arch.

ARCOSOLIUM : Ancient form of tomb, hollowed out of rock beneath an arch.

ARKOSE : Rock composed of quartz and felspar.

ARMARIUM : Cupboard or chest.

ASHLAR : Square, hewn stone.

ASTRAGAL : Small moulding round top or bottom of column.

ATRIUM : Open central Court in Greek and Roman buildings; forecourt in early Christian churches.

BALDACHIN : Canopy, supported on pillars or fastened to wall, over throne, pulpit, altar, etc.

BARBICAN : Outwork defending the entrance to a castle.

BAROQUE : Style with sinuous lines, scrolls and exuberant carved ornaments, named after the painter Federigo Barocci, from Urbino (1528–1612). Born in Rome as a reaction against severe classical Renaissance, it spread throughout Europe.

BARTIZAN : Turret projecting from mediaeval tower.

BASILICA : In mediaeval architecture an aisled church with a clerestory.

BAS-RELIEF : Figures not standing far out from ground on which they are formed.

BATTEN : Long, thin piece of squared timber used for flooring or hanging roof tiles.

BAYS : Internal compartments of a building; each divided from the other not by solid walls but by divisions only marked in the side walls. Also external divisions of a building by fenestration.

BELVEDERE : Raised turret from which to view scenery.

BEMA : Speaker's Tribune, or Platform.

BILLET MOULDING : Ornamental moulding consisting of small cylindrical blocks arranged in a sunken moulding.

BOULEUTERION : Council chamber.

BUCRANE : Sculptured ornament representing ox skull.

BUTTRESS : Projecting support built on to outside of wall.

CABOCHONS : Precious stones polished but not cut into facets.

CADUCEUS : Mercury's wand.

Caldarium: Hot room in Roman baths.

CALOTTE : Skull cap, applied to a detail of this shape.

Camii: Mosque.

CAMPANILE : Isolated bell-tower.

CAPITAL : Moulded or carved top of column.

CARYATID : Whole figure supporting an entablature or other similar member.

CASEMATE : Vaulted chamber in thickness of fortress-wall, with embrasures for defence.

CAVEA : Auditorium of open-air theatre.

CELLA : Main body of a classical temple, excluding the portico.

CENSER : A vessel in which incense is burned.

CENSE : The act of burning incense.

CHALICE : Cup used in Communion service or at Mass.

CHAMFER : Surface produced by bevelling square edge or corner equally on both sides—moulding.

CHAMPLEVÉ ENAMEL : Work in which the metal ground is hollowed out and spaces filled with enamel.

CHAPTER HOUSE : Meeting place of members of religious order.

CHASUBLE : The outer vestment of the celebrant at Mass.

CHEVET : Apsidal east end of church.

CHRESMOGRAPHEION : Chamber for writing down oracles.

CHRISMA : A monogram of Christ formed by the letters χ and ρ.

CIBORIUM : Vessel similar to chalice in which the Host is deposited. Canopy over high altar.

CINQUEFOIL : Arch or circular opening divided into five lobes or leaves by projecting carving.

CIPPUS : Roman term for monumental pillar.

CISTERCIAN : Order founded in 1098 in Burgundy, at Cîteaux (Latin *Cistercium*) near Dijon, and which received a great impulse under St. Bernard, founder of the Abbey of Clairvaux. The monasteries of this Order express by their architecture the severity of the rule (more austere form of Benedictine rule).

CLEPSYDRA : Vessel through which water trickled for the purpose of measuring time.

CLERESTORY : Upper storey with rows of windows.

COFFER : Deep panel in ceiling, vault or dome.

CONSOLE : Ornamental bracket used to support cornices on which to place busts, vases or figures.

COPE : Ecclesiastical vestment worn over surplice.

CORBEL : Block of stone projecting from a wall, supporting some horizontal feature.

CORNICE : Uppermost member of entablature, surmounting the frieze.

COUNTERSCARP : Outer wall or slope of ditch, supporting covered way.

CRENEL : Open space of a battlement.

CROCKET : Carved ornament on angles of spires and on canopies.

CROSSING : That part of a cruciform church where the transepts cross the nave.

CUFIC : Pertaining to Cufa, a town on the Euphrates, south of Babylon; applied especially to an Arabic alphabet earlier employed there.

CULVERIN : Small firearm; large cannon, very long in proportion to its bore, used especially in 16th and 17th centuries.

CUPOLA : Spherical vault or concave ceiling.

CYCLOPEAN : Style of masonry with walls of large, irregular stones, unhewn and uncemented, which in ancient Greece were fabled to be the work of Cyclops, or one-eyed giants.

DIACONICUM : Vestry.

DIAZOMA : Cornice or frieze.

DRIP-STONE : Projecting moulding to throw off rain.

DRUM OR TAMBOUR : Upright part of a cupola.

Enceinte: An enclosing wall of fortifications.

ENGAGED : Built into. ENGAGED COLUMN : Column built into wall.

ENTABLATURE : Arrangements of horizontal members above supporting columns.

ENTASIS : Convex tapering of a column.

EPHEBES : Devotees.

EXEDRA : Apsidal end of a room.

FAÇADE : Face or front of building.

FAÏENCE : Decorated glazed earthenware.

Finial: Ornamental feature placed on top of pinnacle or at base and apex of gable.

Frigidarium: Cold room in Roman bath.

Flamboyant: Late form of the Gothic style, characteristic for its "florid" enrichments of carved ornament, and for the "flaming" arrangements of the window stonefilling.

Fluting: Vertical channelling in the shaft of a column.

Foil: Lobe formed by the cusping of a circle or an arch. Trefoil, quatrefoil, cinquefoil, multifoil, express number of leaf shapes to be seen.

Foliated: Carved with leaf shapes.

Fresco: Painting on plastered wall before plaster has dried.

Frieze: Middle division of a classical entablature.

Gallery: In church architecture, upper storey above an aisle, opened in arches to the nave.

Gallo-Roman: Belonging to the epoch when Gaul was a part of the Roman Empire (1st–4th century).

Glacis: Bank slopping down from fort, on which attackers are without cover from gunfire.

Gothic: Style which appeared in France in the 12th century, and prevailed in Europe from the 13th to the 15th centuries. Its chief elements are the vault with diagonal ribs with pointed arches and flying buttresses.

Groin: Sharp edge at the meeting of two cells of a cross-vault.

Helicoidal: Resembling a snail shell; spiral ornament.

Hieratism: Priestly tradition that made Byzantine art too rigid.

High Gothic: *see* Flamboyant.

Historiated: Adorned with figures.

Hôtel: Large house or mansion, in addition to meaning as in English hotel.

Hypogeum, Hypostyle: Underground room or vault.

Imbricated: Overlapping.

Impluvium: Square basin in the middle of an atrium to receive rainwater.

IMPOST : Brackets in walls, usually formed of mouldings, on which the ends of an arch rest.

In commendum: Ecclesiastical benefice temporarily held in care of clerk.

INTRADOS : Inner curve or underside of an arch.

INTAGLIO : Engraved design; incised carving in hard material.

JAMB : Straight side of an archway, doorway, or window.

JUBE : Screen between nave and chancel (rood-screen).

LANCET : Tall, narrow window with acutely pointed head.

LANTERN : In architecture, a small circular or polygonal turret with windows all round crowning a roof or dome.

LIERNE : Short rib connecting two main ribs.

LINTEL : Horizontal beam or stone bridging an opening.

LOMBARD : Early form of the Romanesque style (9th and 10th centuries) born in Lombardy, Italy.

LOZENGE : Diamond shape.

MACHICOLATION : Projecting gallery or parapet with series of openings for pouring molten substances on attackers below.

MARQUETRY : Inlaid work arranged to form decorative patterns.

MERLON : Part of wall of battlement lying between two openings.

METOPE : The square space between two triglyphs in a frieze of a Doric order.

Mezzo-rilievo: Degree of relief in figures halfway between high and low.

MINIATURE : Painting on a very small scale.

MISERERE : Projection on underside of tilt-up seat in choirstall.

MISERICORD : Room set apart in monastery where monks might take special food as an indulgence: the indulgence or relaxation of monastic rule itself.

MODILLION : Projecting bracket under a cornice in Corinthian and other orders.

MOORISH : Islamic style peculiar to the Moors of Spain (8th–14th century).

MULLION : Vertical bar of wood or stone dividing window into two or more "lights".

NAISKOS : Shrine.

NAOS : Sanctuary or principal chamber of a Greek temple containing the statue of the god.

NARTHEX : In early Christian architecture, a vestibule forming an entrance to a basilica, originally for women penitents and catechumens.

NAUMACHIA : Sea-fight.

NAVE : Body of church.

NEWEL : Central post in circular or winding staircase; also, principal post when flight of stairs meets a landing.

NIMBUS : Bright cloud or halo investing deity or saint.

Nymphaeum: Roman temple of the nymphs.

OCULUS : Circular or "bull's-eye" window.

ODEON : Building for shows.

OGIVE : Pointed arch or window, with double curve.

OMPHALLOA : Conical stone used by oracles.

OPISTHODOME : Enclosed section at rear of a Greek temple sometimes used as a treasury.

Oppidum: Latin for town.

ORDER : In Classical architecture, column with base, shaft, capital, and entablature according to one of the following styles: Greek Doric, Roman Doric, Tuscan Doric, Ionic, Corinthian, Composite. Alternatively an Order of monks.

OVEN-SHAPED : This description is applied to the structures which have the dome shape of the old French bread ovens, e.g. mainly in the case of apses at the eastern end of the church.

PALESTRA : Gymnasium.

PARADOS : Elevation of earth behind fortified place to secure it from rear attack.

PARACCLESION : Chamber for prayer.

PARVIS : Enclosed area in front of church or cathedral.

PATERA : Small flat circular or oval ornament in classical architecture.

PATINA : Encrustation of age to works of art.

PATIO : Courtyard.

PEDIMENT : Low-pitched gable used in Classical, Renaissance, and neo-classical architecture above a portico.

PENDENTIVE : Spherical triangle formed between each pair of supporting arches in dome resting on square base.

PERISTYLE : Row of columns round building or courtyard.

PILASTER : Flat column against face of wall.

PINNACLE : Ornamental form crowning a spire, tower, buttress.

PISCINA : Basin for washing the Communion or Mass vessels.

PODIUM : Continuous base of plinth supporting columns.

POLYPTYCH : Picture or carving with many panels.

POROS : Chalky stone.

PORTAL : Gate or doorway.

PREDELLA : In an altar-piece the horizontal strip below the main representation, often used for a number of subsidiary representations in a row.

PRESBYTERY : Part of church reserved for clergy, also dwelling house for clergy.

PRITANAEUM : Public hall.

PRONAOS : Vestibule of a Greek or Roman temple, enclosed by side walls and a range of columns in front.

PROPYLAEA : Entrance gateway to an enclosure.

PROSCENIUM : In a Greek or Roman theatre, the stage on which the action took place.

PROTHESIS : Credence table for Eucharist.

PSALTER : Book of Psalms.

Putto (plural *putti*): Small naked boy.

PYXIS : Sacred box containing Host after consecration.

RAMPART : Defensive bank of earth, with or without stone parapet.

RELIQUARIES : Chests or caskets containing relics.

ROCOCO : Late Baroque style with a profusion of rock-like forms, scrolls, crimped shells (from French "rocaille"—"rock work").

ROMANESQUE : Architectural style prevalent in Western Europe towards the end of 12th century, characterised by use of massive stone vaulting and the round-headed arch. Usually known in reference to English buildings as Norman.

ROOD-SCREEN : Open screen across chancel entrance in church.

ROSE-WINDOW : Gothic circular window filled with tracery resembling a rose.

ROTUNDA : Circular building, usually with domed roof.

RUPESTRAL : Rock.

SACRISTY : Part of church where sacred vessels and vestments are kept.

SARCOPHAGUS : Stone receptacle for corpse.

SERPENTINE : Decorative stone.

SOFFIT : Underside of lintel, arch or cornice.

SPRINGER : Bottom stone of arch.

SQUINCH : Small stone arch across an interior angle of square tower to support octagonal spire.

STELE : Upright monument.

STEREOTOMY : Art or science of cutting stones into regular forms.

STOA : Detached colonnade.

STRINGCOURSE : Projecting horizontal moulding or projecting course of stone or brick running across face of building.

STUCCO : Plaster work.

STYLOBATE : Substructure on which a colonnade stands.

SUDATORIUM : Room for hot-air baths to produce sweating.

SYNTHRONON : Enthronement.

TELAMONES : Carved male figures serving as pillars.

TEMENOS : Sacred precinct.

TEPIDARIUM : Room for warm bath.

TESSERA : Small cube of glass, stone or marble used in mosaic.

TIERCERON : Secondary rib, issuing from main springer or central boss and leading to a ridge rib.

TORUS : Moulding in base of columns with semi-circular profile.

TRACHYTE : Rough-surfaced.

TRANSEPT : Transverse portion of a cross-shaped church.

TRANSOM : Horizontal bar across the openings of a window.

TRIBUNAL : Confessional.

TRIBUNE : Gallery of church.

TRIFORIUM: Arcaded wall passage or blank arcading facing the nave at the height of the roof of the side-aisle and below the clerestory windows.

TRIGLYPHS: Blocks with vertical grooves separating the metopes in a doric frieze.

TRIPTYCH: Picture or carving on three panels.

TUFA: Rock of cellular texture of volcanic origin.

TYMPANUM: Triangular space between sloping and horizontal cornices above lintel of doorway.

VOLUTE: Spiral scroll.

WAGON-ROOF: Roof in which by closely set rafters with arched braces the appearance of the inside of a canvas tilt over a wagon is achieved.

INDEX OF TOWNS AND PLACES VISITED